SCHOLARLY COMMUNICATION

SCHOLARLY COMMUNICATION

The Report of the National Enquiry

THE JOHNS HOPKINS UNIVERSITY PRESS
BALTIMORE AND LONDON

The Johns Hopkins University Press, Baltimore, Maryland 21218
The Johns Hopkins Press Ltd., London

Library of Congress Catalog Number 79–51420
ISBN 0–8018–2267–X hardcover
ISBN 0–8018–2268–8 paperback

Contents

Preface

In late 1973 several directors of university presses met with officials of the National Endowment for the Humanities to discuss what they felt to be the increasingly serious problems with which scholarly publishers were faced. As a result, the American Council of Learned Societies (ACLS) was asked to sponsor a conference on the publication and dissemination of scholarship in the United States in order to determine the possible value of conducting a thorough study of the subject. The Council readily agreed to do so, and the Endowment provided funds to bring together some thirty-five scholars, publishers, editors of learned journals, officers of learned societies, directors of research libraries, and foundation and government officials in June 1974. Following this, and a second conference held in the fall, a committee was appointed to prepare a detailed proposal for an enquiry into the creation and dissemination of scholarly knowledge, with special concern for the humanities and humanistic social sciences.

The committee met regularly in the succeeding months and submitted a proposal to the conference group for their consideration in the spring of 1975. Upon approval by that group, financing for the National Enquiry was successfully sought from the National Endowment for the Humanities, the Ford Foundation, the Andrew W. Mellon Foundation, and the Rockefeller Foundation. A widely representative, autonomous board of governors was appointed; the staff were selected; an office was set up in Princeton; and the Enquiry was officially begun in January 1976. It was understood from the first that the final report of the Enquiry would be presented under the aegis of the board of governors, not of the American Council of Learned Societies or of the funding agencies.

Thanks are due to Edward E. Booher, director of the Enquiry from its inception in 1976 to its penultimate phase in the summer of 1978, and to the technical director, Nazir Bhagat. Most of the report here presented is based on the planning, consulting, and research undertaken by them and their staff, Robert A. Forrest, Robert S. Hohwald, and Judith Mischka.

David W. Breneman of the Brookings Institution and Herbert C. Morton of Resources for the Future, both members of the board, conducted further interviews and research, and wrote this report. The board is deeply grateful to them for undertaking this work at a crucial point and bringing it to, as we believe, a successful conclusion. They were assisted by a steering committee composed of board members Herbert S. Bailey, Jr., Warren J. Haas, Chester Kerr, R. M. Lumiansky, and Gordon N. Ray. Mr. Bailey wrote the Epilogue to chapter 1. Thomas A. Noble of the ACLS staff contributed substantially to the development and completion of the project.

A number of other members of the board also made helpful suggestions, as did several outside readers, including Suzanne D. Frankie, Marilyn Gaull, Janet D. Griffith, Marie R. Hansen, Arthur Herschman, Roland Hoover, Joseph Raben, Hans Rütimann, and Robert Shirrell. Jo Hinkel edited the report, and Florence Robinson prepared the index. Ellen Pyda and Susanne Sullivan typed the manuscript.

It remains to express appreciation to the American Council of Learned Societies for its sponsorship of the Enquiry, to the four foundations whose material support made it possible, and to the many consultants and other experts in various aspects of scholarly communication whose interest and advice were essential to the production of the report.

We believe that the recommendations make sense. Let us hope they will lead to improvements beneficial to all concerned with the creation and dissemination of scholarly knowledge.

The Board of Governors of the National Enquiry

Foreword

For those of us who have been most closely connected with this National Enquiry into Scholarly Communication, the journey which ends with this report has been quite lengthy and at times a bit bumpy. We are convinced, however, that our recommendations point the way toward the types of changes that must be made during the next decade or so if humanistic scholarship is to continue to flourish.

During the period of the Enquiry we came to realize more clearly than any of us had earlier realized the truth of one axiom: the various constituencies involved in scholarly communication—the scholars themselves, the publishers of books and of learned journals, the research librarians, the learned societies—are all components of a single system and are thus fundamentally dependent upon each other. Moreover, we found that this single system in all its parts is highly sensitive to influence from two outside factors—the actions of the funding agencies, and the developments of the new technologies.

Given this interdependence among the various components and influences within the system for scholarly communication, it follows that the numerous problems which the system faces can be effectively solved only if the individuals working within one part of the system are fully mindful of the other parts before decisions are taken. What is called for, therefore, is markedly increased consultation among the leaders in the various components and influences. Let us hope that ways can be found to make such give-and-take a regular practice in the process of decision making. Further, for such consultation to be fully effective we need a far better collection of hard facts about each of the components than the workers in this Enquiry found available or could assemble. Thus we are all hoping that the National Endowment for the Humanities will take our recommendation seriously and establish an on-going fact-finding center for scholarly communication.

The scholars themselves are of course the central figures in our system: the basic reason for the system is to help them carry out their work. It is appropriate, therefore, that the following words be addressed to them.

Since humanistic scholars work primarily with books and journals, and since a considerable part of their time is spent browsing in research libraries, they may find the view of the future presented in the Epilogue to Chapter 1 alarming. Let it be clearly stated here, therefore, that no one connected with this National Enquiry has any desire to see books and journals disappear, or browsing in research libraries decrease. Rather, our hope is that the new technology can be so used as to increase the effectiveness with which the other components in the system rapidly and reliably serve the needs of the scholars. In the last analysis, it is their work which counts.

R. M. Lumiansky
Chairman, Board of Governors

xiii

THE AMERICAN COUNCIL OF LEARNED SOCIETIES

The American Council of Learned Societies, which sponsored the Enquiry, is a private nonprofit federation of forty-two national scholarly organizations concerned with the humanities and the humanistic aspects of the social sciences.

The purpose of the Council, as set forth in its constitution, is "the advancement of humanistic studies in all fields of learning and the maintenance and strengthening of relations among the national societies devoted to such studies." The Council, consisting of a thirteen-member Board of Directors and one delegate from each of the constituent societies, meets annually. The Board of Directors usually holds bimonthly meetings, except during the summer. The work of the Council is carried on by an executive staff with the help of an extensive system of committees.

The American Council of Learned Societies was organized in 1919 and incorporated in the District of Columbia in 1924. Its offices are located at 345 East Forty-Sixth Street, New York City.

SCHOLARLY COMMUNICATION

CHAPTER 1

Overview and Principal Recommendations

The National Enquiry into Scholarly Communication was initiated in 1975 in response to the widespread concern in the academic community that a crisis in finance threatened the performance of research libraries and the viability of scholarly publishing. Fewer copies of new books were being sold, prices of scholarly books and journals were increasing rapidly, acquisition budgets of research libraries were falling far behind these increases, and libraries were shifting their expenditures from book to journal purchases.

Scholarly publishers—particularly university press directors—feared that declining unit sales would lead to still higher selling prices, which might reduce sales further, and that a growing number of high-quality but specialized manuscripts would go unpublished unless subsidized.

Editors of scholarly journals, particularly in the humanities and social sciences, faced an equally uncertain future because of their dependence on library subscriptions and the poor prospect for increasing individual subscriptions during a slowdown in the growth of college and university faculties and of graduate programs.

Librarians in the major research centers were facing the difficult task of allocating increasingly scarce dollars among the vast and steadily growing numbers of books, journals, microforms, and other materials of scholarship. No longer able to develop or maintain comprehensive, self-contained collections, they were searching for new ways to organize limited resources in order best to serve the needs of teaching and research. The proliferation of journals, coupled with their sharply rising prices, posed a particularly vexing problem for librarians.

While echoing the worries of publishers and librarians about rising prices and declining library budgets, scholars were also concerned about backlogs of accepted journal articles, leading to discouraging publication delays. For younger scholars, seeking recognition and facing decisions on

tenure in a steadily worsening academic market, publishing delays meant far
more than simple irritation—careers were at stake. Meanwhile, for reasons
linked to both the economic pressures facing publishers and the labor-market
pressures felt by faculty, two seemingly contradictory charges were heard:
First, that too many books and journals of marginal quality and usefulness
were being published; and, second, that works of considerable scholarly
value were failing to find outlets.

Further complicating the picture were the claims being made on behalf
of new technology for libraries and publishing. Some experts argued that
books and journals were nearing obsolescence and would be replaced by
various electronic storage and retrieval systems. Libraries would cease to be
storehouses for the printed word, becoming instead service centers (or
modules) in the new information networks. Home and office computers,
linked to cathode-ray tubes for viewing, would become the information
centers of the future. The effect of these prophecies, some presumably based
in fact, some in fancy, was to raise the level of uncertainty about how to cope
with the difficulties plaguing the existing system of scholarly communication.

Finally, officials in federal and state governments and in private foundations were uncertain about the roles they should play in responding to cries
for help from the various sectors of the system. Should emphasis be placed
on title subsidies at university presses, or should grants be made to research
libraries to foster unique collections? How much should be invested in
maintaining or strengthening the current system, and how much in developing and implementing new technology? To what extent, and in what areas,
should market forces be relied upon as the surest guide to acceptable
outcomes, and where does market failure occur, requiring public—or private—intervention? What types of intervention are compatible with—and
which are inimical to—academic and intellectual freedom?

This complex of questions, involving scholars, learned societies, book
and journal publishers, research libraries, technology, and foundation and
government policies, gave rise to the investigation and recommendations
reported here. Initially, the National Enquiry envisioned a study encompass-
ing the entire domain of scholarly publishing. But as the investigation
proceeded, it became clear that the focus would have to be limited to the
humanities and related social sciences. Thus, while the report examines
some areas of scholarly communication in general—for example, the circumstances of research libraries—its discussion of book and journal publish-

ing is restricted largely to the humanistic disciplines. Although separate chapters are devoted to scholarly books, scholarly journals, and research libraries, the emphasis throughout the study was not on the problems of each group in isolation, but on their interrelationships. The first chapter presents principal findings, conclusions, and recommendations for the system of scholarly communication as a whole; succeeding chapters describe and document in more detail the research on which the conclusions are based, and include more specific recommendations for the publishing, library, and scholarly communities.

THE CRISIS REDEFINED

As the preceding discussion suggests, the sum of many partial views created a sense of impending crisis in the mid-1970s. Many observers believed that the handful of university press closings in the early 1970s marked the beginning of a trend, and the cancellation of journal subscriptions by several university libraries under stress was seen as a portent of more drastic cutbacks. Most of the information that people had, particularly about humanities and social science publishing, was anecdotal or specific only to a given institution. In the absence of more complete information, it is understandable that an exaggerated sense of desperation developed.

The evidence presented in the following chapters supports the need to redefine the crisis as less dramatic than was earlier thought, but more persistent and difficult to handle. In fact, the term *crisis* in its precise meaning as a turning point, a crucial time or event, is misleading when applied to our topic, for the problems facing scholarly communication are of a different nature, not dramatic enough to kill the patient, but able, if left unattended, to produce a lingering, wasting disease. Scholarly communication will clearly persist, but presses, journals, and research libraries cannot be sheltered from changing economic conditions. The challenge now, as at any time, is to adapt intelligently to new circumstances.

Briefly stated, our investigation supports the following redefinition of the issues and problems facing scholarly communication in the humanities and social sciences:

1. As readers, scholars report a high degree of satisfaction with the existing system of scholarly communication. The high prices of books and their occasional unavailability in the university library are common complaints, but in general, scholars are satisfied with library services and with the quality and availability of books and journals.

2. As authors rather than as readers, scholars have more complaints about the system. Pressures to publish for professional advancement are strongly felt and generally accepted; however, the view is widespread that quantity matters more than quality, a situation that many scholars resent. Refereeing is often viewed as too slow, and younger scholars express doubts about the fairness of that system. The delay from journal acceptance to publication is seen as a problem, particularly when career advancement is at stake. (The impact of delays on the course of scholarship is less clear.) The number of humanities and social science journals currently in existence, however, is thought to be adequate.

3. There is little evidence that meritorious journal or book manuscripts fail to be published, although submission to several publishers is often required. (Title subsidies provided by private foundations and more recently by the National Endowment for the Humanities are essential to achieving this end, however.) Scholars are also concerned about the opposite possibility—lax standards and proliferation of mediocre books and journals.

4. The number of scholarly presses and journals that have gone out of business in recent years is miniscule, indicating that scholarly publishing has greater resiliency than many observers thought.

5. Prices for scholarly books and for scientific and technical journals have continued to climb rapidly, while subscription rates for many humanities and social science journals have risen much more slowly. Unit sales for the average scholarly book have fallen sharply in recent years.

6. Library acquisition budgets continue to lag behind increases in volume and costs of scholarly materials. The shift in library expenditures from books to journals, first noted between 1969 and 1973, continued as sharply between 1973 and 1976.

7. Resource sharing among libraries, primarily through interlibrary loan, encounters growing obstacles as libraries doing the lending are less willing to absorb the associated costs.

8. Technological advances have occurred in parts of the system (for example, word processing and computerized preparation of camera-ready copy for book and journal production and development of computer-based bibliographic networks), but there is little evidence to support the view that books and journals will be rendered technologically obsolete, or that computers will revolutionize the management of libraries. User resistance to the substitution of microfilm or microfiche for books remains strong.

What emerges from this summary is a mixed picture of a basically healthy communication system beset with numerous problems, none of them fatal, but requiring a variety of improvements if the system is to continue to achieve its purposes. A particularly interesting finding is that those who operate the scholarly network—librarians, book publishers, and journal editors—are much more concerned about the state of scholarly communication than are the scholars themselves in the humanities and related social sciences. Why this is so cannot be definitively answered, but some possible explanations come to mind.

1. Librarians, publishers, and editors have done a good job of coping with the problems that have become increasingly difficult in recent years— better probably than they have realized. The responses of scholars to the Enquiry questionnaires seem to bear out this conclusion.

2. Scholars' opinions are based primarily on the service they are receiving, not on an understanding of the difficulties of providing the service or an awareness of greater difficulties ahead, and it is apprehension about the dimensions of future needs that troubles librarians and publishers. The reasons for their concerns are discussed in subsequent sections of the report.

3. The Enquiry's survey of scholars' attitudes focused on the humanities and related social sciences. In these areas, the need for very rapid service and the ability to scan enormous bibliographies at will do not exist in the same measure as they do in scientific and technical disciplines. We do not have a comparable survey of the opinions of users of scientific and technical journals. Nevertheless, it would be erroneous to conclude that scientific scholars are less satisfied, since it is in the sciences that the greatest advances in harnessing new technology to bibliographic needs have been made.

There is also an interesting parallel in our redefinition of the problems with similar experiences in recent years in the financing of higher education. The sense of disaster—of impending crisis—expressed by those concerned with scholarly communication, was echoed during the early 1970s by those who shared comparable concerns regarding the future of graduate education or the plight of small, private colleges. In both cases, the immediate sense of crisis, triggered by a sharp and unexpected change in economic fortune, gave way to an understanding that most programs and institutions would endure, but that solutions would not be simple, quickly achieved, or ever complete. Since the main groups that make up the system of scholarly communication—scholars, presses, journals, and libraries—are largely part of higher education, it is not surprising that the pattern found in other studies of financing higher education during the 1970s should be repeated here. If the parallel holds, then we should not expect neat or simple solutions to the problems of scholarly communication; instead, the recommendations in this report are but the latest in a continuing series of assessments that will be necessary as the system evolves and the problems and issues change.

PERSPECTIVES, GOALS, AND RATIONALE FOR FINANCING

The objective of the National Enquiry is the improvement of scholarly communication, conceived as a system embracing a number of interacting and interdependent groups. Each group shares this ultimate objective: Scholars want the best research to be widely publicized and shared, directors of scholarly presses and editors of scholarly journals want to publish works of highest quality and disseminate their publications widely, and librarians seek to develop comprehensive collections and make them easily accessible. Nonetheless, they may adopt conflicting strategies in approaching specific problems. A pertinent example is the continuing conflict between publishers and librarians over limits to be set on photocopying, with librarians emphasizing rapid, convenient, and low-cost dissemination and publishers emphasizing the economic necessity to sell the published product in order to sustain themselves, their authors, and the publishing function. A second example is the disagreement between publishers and librarians over the purpose and justification for differential pricing of journal subscriptions, with higher rates being charged to libraries than to individuals. As these examples show, what is good for book or journal publishers may not be good for libraries, and vice versa. Comparable conflicts arise throughout the system—between authors and publishers, faculty members and librarians, and publishers and foundations. And yet, despite these inevitable conflicts, the binding forces, the common interests, are ultimately stronger. Each group, each activity, is essential to all others; should one part fail, the others could not function.

What distinguishes the National Enquiry from other studies that have concentrated primarily on one part of the system—libraries, presses, periodicals—is the effort to study and understand the perspectives of each group, in order to build on the common interests that all have in sustaining and improving the system of scholarly communication. Our principal recommendations at the end of this chapter draw on the Enquiry's studies and analyses of each sector, reported in greater detail in subsequent chapters, and on the broader perspective that derives from the effort to understand the system as a whole.

An appropriate starting point is to identify the characteristics of an effective system of scholarly communication, applicable to all disciplines. From this statement of goals, we proceed to the formulation of a rationale for financing that distinguishes areas where self-help is both possible and desirable from those that require the assistance of others.

An effective system of scholarly communication should meet the following objectives:

Access. Readers should have access to a comprehensive bibliographic system that allows them to identify and locate material and to obtain it at a reasonable cost and without excessive delay.

Entry. Authors should find a variety of book publishers and journal editors willing to give a manuscript a fair reading and committed to a decision based on scholarly merit.

Quality control. The system should have the capacity to differentiate between works of greater and lesser quality, of greater and lesser importance, and to match the form of publication to these differences.

Timeliness. Manuscripts should be accepted or rejected promptly, and works should be published on schedule. Advance announcements should keep scholars apprised of forthcoming books and articles, and distribution systems should make completed work available rapidly.

Coordination. The participants in the communications venture—scholars, publishers, technologists, scholarly societies, government and foundations, and libraries—should be mindful of their obligations and their interdependence, and pursue their goals in light of the effects their actions have on others and on the entire system.

Adaptability. Since the needs of scholars, the tools of scholarship, the uses of knowledge, and the economic and social environment are constantly changing, the scholarly community should maintain a responsive attitude toward the elimination of obsolete methods and materials and toward possibilities of productive innovation.

Financial viability. Financing arrangements should ensure the economic viability of each function essential to the system of scholarly communication.

As the last item suggests, appropriate financing is essential if the scholarly system is to meet these objectives. Knowledge, the substance of scholarly communication, is a public good in the sense that one person's acquisition of it does not diminish the amount available for others, and indeed, may ultimately enhance it. The private marketplace cannot be relied upon to produce the socially optimal amount of such public goods, and thus subsidies of one form or another are generally required for their production. A variety of subsidies and other nonmarket procedures are both necessary and already in use to secure acceptable performance from—and for—the scholarly enterprise:

- Research and scholarship are supported by public and private grants, and released time of scholars from teaching is underwritten and contributed to the research effort by universities and other organizations.

- Research libraries are supported through university budgets and by other public and private sources, rather than by income from fees that cover acquisition and operating costs.

- University presses are supported to varying degrees by their institutions, and their publication of individual books often requires title subsidies.

- Research libraries contribute to the support of journals by providing a substantial and stable core of subscribers for specialized journals, many of them priced beyond the means of individual subscribers.

- Academic journals are often subsidized by the universities or scholarly societies that sponsor them, and by individuals who volunteer their time.

- The evaluation and selection of articles and manuscripts (an essential service to scholars and to promotion and tenure committees) is largely provided free of charge or with minimal reader fees through the editorial offices and selection procedures of presses and journals.

These several forms of subsidy to the production and dissemination of knowledge—outright grants, contributed time and facilities, volunteer efforts—have helped to ensure that a far greater body of scholarship exists than would have been possible in their absence. The need for subsidy, however, should not obscure the fact that large parts of the system do function through market transactions, including sales to individual consumers. University presses sell their books to libraries and to individuals, and journals do the same with subscriptions. Under certain conditions, journals receive payment from libraries or from individuals for photocopies made of articles, and the newly created Copyright Clearance Center expedites such payments. Many journals, particularly in scientific and technical fields, levy page charges or submission fees, and more research libraries are introducing fees for such services as interlibrary loan. Thus, the observation that knowledge is a public good must be qualified by the recognition that, when embodied in the form of books and journals or library services, it is fully capable of being produced in discrete units and sold to private individuals, much like any other commodity.

The ability to impose charges for specific products or services that are part of the system of scholarly communication has several implications for policy. First, it means that questions of subsidy are inherently complex and not amenable to simple answers. User charges that cover partial or full costs become an option, and thus subsidy is not an all or nothing proposition. Research libraries, for example, have traditionally tried to minimize user charges for bibliographic services, interlibrary loan, and similar services to scholars; however, such charges are clearly feasible, and cannot be ruled out of consideration. Second, and closely related, the wider the applicability of user charges, the wider the scope for self-help within the system. There need be no automatic presumption, for example, that a journal faced with falling subscriptions or rapidly rising costs requires new or additional subsidies; instead, possibilities such as introducing submission fees, merger, or takeover by a stronger agency must be considered, along with the option of permitting the journal to cease publication. Third, the mix of public or private subsidy and user charges may, of necessity, change over time. Research libraries, in particular, have played a key financial role for many years in helping journals and scholarly presses cover a large share of their costs by purchasing hardbound books in preference to paperbacks and by paying higher institutional subscription rates. The financial strains that have hit higher education generally in this decade, and which seem likely to persist and even worsen in the next, have forced a reexamination of these acquisition policies. Librarians have no choice but to search for new ways to make best use of limited budgets, and several of the Enquiry's recommendations are directed to that end. Creation of a national periodicals center, for example (see Recommendation Two), will provide libraries with an alternative to subscribing to seldom-used journals. This change, in turn, will force journal editors to seek new markets, new sources of revenue, or new ways of publishing that reduce costs.

Apart from future changes that may be necessary, there are several aspects of current financing that are questionable and call for rethinking:

- In virtually all academic fields there is a price differential between the subscription rate charged to individuals and to institutions. In humanities and social science disciplines this differential is small and no source of concern, but in physical science, mathematics, engineering, and other technical disciplines, the differences are considerable, with institutional rates often set at several times the individual rate. With differences this large, it is hard to avoid the conclusion that some publishers are taking advantage of the captive market represented by libraries. Given the prospect of severely limited library acquisition budgets for a decade or more, such pricing practices are unlikely to be in the long-run best interests of the scientific community, including the journal publishers.

- Libraries have traditionally sought to avoid user charges for most services, but the tighter budgets that have marked recent years should force a reassessment of that policy. If the alternatives are to eliminate a service, such as interlibrary loan or bibliographic searches, or charge for it, charging would be preferable.

- Private foundations and government agencies that support research are often unwilling to assist in supporting the publication and related costs required to disseminate the findings which result. Since much of the value, or purpose, of research is lost if others are not made aware of it, foundation and government officials should reexamine their policies toward the support of publication and related costs.

- The relative ease with which new journals can be started is a strength of the scholarly enterprise, but there is greater need now to consider also the costs imposed on the total communication system. The prevailing view among scholars surveyed by the Enquiry is that enough journals are currently published, and each new journal puts added stress on library budgets. Ease of entry, therefore, should be matched by ease of exit; journals that fail to maintain their readership should be permitted—even encouraged—to cease publication. Libraries, in particular, need to be discriminating in their subscriptions, basing decisions on studies of journal usage.

A general guideline that has influenced the recommendations in this report emerges from the discussion set forth above and from the Enquiry's research and subsequent redefinition of the "crisis." In our view, increased government or foundation outlays should be concentrated primarily on efforts and activities that promise improvement for the *system* of scholarly communication. Examples of systemwide improvements that require external financial support are the national bibliographic system (Recommendation One) and the national periodicals center (Recommendation Two). Developments of this sort will not come about unaided or as a natural consequence of current operations, even though the benefits are substantial. Instead, these systemwide capabilities are a form of social overhead capital designed to improve scholarly communication, but requiring public investment or private philanthropy for their realization. By contrast, wherever possible, our recommendations stress self-help from within the system, including increased use of manuscript submission fees, collaboration among scholarly publishers, new initiatives by learned societies, cooperation with the Copyright Clearance Center, support for scholarly publishing from universities without presses, and improved marketing of scholarly books abroad. Throughout, we have assumed that new sources of external support for scholarly communication will be limited, and this assumption has led to recommendations that place heavy reliance on improved management and more efficient forms of organization, coupled with an emphasis on identifying the highest priority uses for new resources that do become available.

THE CENTRAL CONCLUSION

The extraordinary growth of the scholarly enterprise during the last two decades requires important qualitative changes in the way certain scholarly materials are published, disseminated, stored, and made available. Although the changes recommended in this report are evolutionary, not revolutionary, and will require in some instances public and private subsidies to implement, the goal to be pursued is not a continuation of business as usual, but rather the development of new ways to meet the needs of scholarship. Our recommendations stress the immediate, short-term actions that should be taken, and a speculative discussion of the long-term development of the system is presented at the end of this chapter.

Statistics cited in subsequent chapters document the remarkable growth in the number of scholarly studies published, nationally and internationally, in the last two decades. Growth rates such as these, whether measured by number of books and articles published, new journals created, library acquisitions, or the dollar value of expenditures, could not have been sustained indefinitely, even in the absence of financial pressures on library budgets. Financial problems, primarily within the universities, forced attention earlier and more sharply to the issues that have concerned the Enquiry, but the difficulties of financing, managing, and rendering useful the vastly enlarged body of scholarly materials would have arisen inevitably, if less dramatically, from the sheer pressures of increased size.

It is true that many of the financial problems (but not necessarily the problems of performance) that plague the system could be eliminated through sharply increased subsidies for libraries, journals, and scholarly presses that would allow each group to continue its activities unchanged. Such a "solution" is not only unrealistic and counter to the rationale for financing stated earlier, but even if possible, would be a serious mistake. The sheer size and rapid growth of scholarly and research material in all disciplines have created problems of performance that cannot be solved simply by more stable financing of current practice. A review of the objectives that an effective system of scholarly communication should meet—access, entry, quality control, timeliness, coordination, adaptability—suggests that several of them can only be satisfactorily achieved by creating new capabilities within the communication system. Rapid growth of scholarly material puts a premium on up-to-date, comprehensive, bibliographic services that allow scholars to identify and locate essential books and articles; however, in many areas of specialized research, and particularly in the humanities and social sciences, such computer-based bibliographic systems do not exist. Rapid growth and a greatly enlarged scale of activities have also created—or contributed to—problems of quality control and timeliness of publication. Greater use of new forms of publication—"on-demand," synoptic, and microform—may be one answer to these problems by providing publishers and editors with more options for placing manuscripts into the communications network. The success of a more differentiated system for publishing—or recording—the results of scholarship, however, will depend critically upon the accompanying bibliographic capability, since an item stored on a microform or in a computer memory bank is of little use if it cannot be located.

As these examples demonstrate, quantitative changes in the scholarly enterprise, quite apart from financial considerations, have created a need for qualitative changes in the methods of scholarly communication. Rapid growth has posed the most immediate and pressing problems for the nation's research libraries, and finding ways to help librarians cope intelligently with the flood of material engulfing them is central to any rational solution to the problems of scholarly communication. These institutions, so indispensable to students and researchers, are also essential to the market for scholarly books and journals. Thus, changes in their acquisition policies will have pronounced effects on the fortunes of scholarly publishers and on the quality of service provided to scholars and students. For reasons spelled out in chapter 4, however, the day of the comprehensive, self-contained library, if it ever existed, is irrevocably past. Anyone concerned with improving scholarly communication has no realistic alternative but to support efforts that will provide librarians with more effective ways to allocate increasingly scarce resources. The first three recommendations in this report are designed with that purpose in mind.

The growth in the number of journals published, and their rapidly escalating subscription rates, particularly in scientific and technical fields, pose an especially serious problem for libraries. Interlibrary loan as a method of resource-sharing has been relied upon increasingly to extend the reach of individual libraries, but it has encountered growing resistance, particularly from the dozen or so largest libraries that receive the bulk of the requests. Several of these libraries have recently introduced stiff fees for lending, in part to cover costs, and in part to discourage requests. Creation of a national periodicals center, as described in Recommendation Two, will remove much of the pressure from interlibrary loan and will provide libraries with a reliable source from which to obtain copies of articles from journals too seldom used to warrant library subscription. The existence of a national periodicals center will also reduce the number of back issues that each library must keep, thus relieving the pressure for expansion of library buildings. Payments to publishers through the Copyright Clearance Center for photocopies made in excess of established guidelines will also be handled much more efficiently through the periodicals center, relieving libraries of much of the bookkeeping burden.

Coupled with development of a nationwide, computer-based bibliographic system, the creation of a national periodicals center will lead to a changing environment for journal publishers, particularly in scientific and technical disciplines. On the one hand, librarians will have a new option to consider in addition to subscribing or relying on interlibrary loan, and presumably some will exercise that option by canceling subscriptions to seldom-used periodicals. On the other hand, the capacity created in the periodicals center should increase the market for alternative forms of publication, including on-demand production of either microform copies or paper and print copies of articles stored in microform, and synoptic or abstract publishing, in which journal abstracts are published with full copies available on demand. In a sense, the periodicals center will become a service and fulfillment center for these types of publications, thereby strengthening their economic base.

For several reasons, the impact of the periodicals center should be most pronounced in the scientific and technical disciplines rather than in the humanities. First, subscription rates for scientific journals are far higher than they are in the humanities, so library budgetary savings from cancellations will be greater there. Second, there is often a premium on speed of publication and access in scientific fields, and the periodicals center and improved bibliographic service will increase the attraction of using new forms of publication for many scientific research findings. Third, the market for scientific and technical materials is much broader than for the humanities, since many commercial firms follow the scientific literature. The National Technical Information Service in Springfield, Virginia, for example, operated until recently an article photocopying service covering a subset of scientific journals of interest primarily to commercial clients; the periodicals center could provide a similar service, and expand beyond it.

Whether the periodicals center is created or not (and if it is, it will not be fully operational for several years), highly specialized journals in all disciplines with small numbers of subscribers will be increasingly vulnerable to library cancellations. Thus, regardless of the outcome of the recommendation for a periodicals center, it behooves journal editors, scholarly societies, and concerned scholars to seek new ways to expand journal revenues and cut costs. In our view, continued net growth in the number of journals published should be discouraged, and thus we recommend that subsidies not be used to prop up failing journals (Recommendation Four). Cost savings are clearly possible, however, by contracting out production, subscription fulfillment, and other noneditorial services to larger, more professional organizations (Recommendation Five). We also recommend that journals cooperate with the program of the Copyright Clearance Center, established in response to revisions in the copyright law (Recommendation Six). In addition, the discussion of journals in chapter 2 contains several suggestions regarding new sources of revenue and improved management practices.

Although much has been written about the merits of on-demand publication—or recording—of book-length manuscripts, our conclusion is that such a development would do relatively little to improve the system of scholarly communication. Although the number of scholarly books published in this country has increased steadily over the years, the explosive growth and most severe cost increases have occurred with journals. Reducing the number of scholarly books published in traditional form would yield little, if any, benefit to the scholarly community, nor would it do much to reduce the acquisition problems facing libraries. As is evident from their behavior, librarians are more willing to reduce book purchases than to cancel journal subscriptions, making it more critical to provide librarians with options to reduce journal subscriptions rather than book purchases. Indeed, if the periodicals center is successful, reduced pressure on library budgets for journal subscriptions and for storage may allow increased book purchases.

For scholarly book publishing, our principal recommendations center on ways to increase book sales by more vigorous efforts to promote sales abroad; on ways to broaden support for publication through selective title subsidies and cooperative ventures with universities without presses; and on ways to cut costs through joint operations, service contracts, or mergers. Details of these proposals are spelled out in Recommendations Seven through Ten, and in chapter 3 on scholarly books.

Recognizing that the system of scholarly communication will continue to face problems of finance and of performance not currently foreseen, and that the recommendations advanced here, if carried out, will not solve all existing problems and will have unanticipated consequences, our final recommendations call for creation of an office of scholarly communication and for a standing committee of scholars, publishers, and librarians. An office of scholarly communication, within the National Endowment for the Humanities, would be charged with providing ongoing information and analyses on the state of scholarly communication, would be an early warning system for impending problems, and would be a source of ideas for their solution. The standing committee, to be organized by the American Council of Learned Societies, the Association of American University Presses, and the Association of Research Libraries, would serve as a forum for discussion of the intelligent use of new technology in publishing and library operations.

Twelve of the Enquiry's recommendations have been selected for emphasis in this chapter. The first ten, together with several additional recommendations, are discussed as well in the body of the report. Recommendations One and Two—which are systemwide in their impact—and Recommendation Three are discussed in the context of the needs of research libraries in chapter 4. Recommendations Four through Six are further developed in chapter 2 on scholarly journals, and Seven through Ten in chapter 3 on scholarly books and presses. A brief Afterword highlights the significance of Recommendations Three, Eleven, and Twelve in creating a continuing capacity to pursue a systems approach to the further development of scholarly communication.

Recommendation One: A national bibliographic system

We recommend that research libraries, scholarly associations, and organizations currently engaged in producing bibliographic services join with the Library of Congress in creating a linked, national bibliographic system.

An ideal bibliographic system would permit scholars to identify information pertinent to their work and indicate how and where that information can be most readily obtained. This ideal is far from being realized, however, even for scholars with direct access to a major research library. For those who must depend on smaller libraries, access to many existing publications is effectively foreclosed.

Fortunately, the development of computerized bibliographic systems promises to expand access to scholarly materials dramatically by freeing users from dependence on the local library collection and card catalog as the source of information on books, serials, and other materials. A variety of bibliographic data bases have been created in recent years, covering specific fields of inquiry such as medicine, languages, and agriculture, or serving libraries in a specific state or region. The task ahead is to build upon these efforts by linking them together into an accessible bibliographic system that will serve the members of the research community, regardless of a scholar's field of study or location. Such a system will also help in the internal operations of libraries, making it possible to improve their performance.

Forging a national bibliographic system from the many elements already in existence plus the creation of new components will be a multiyear job, replete with tedious and time-consuming technical and operating details that must be worked out in a cooperative manner. A promising start has been made under the leadership of the Council of Library Resources, which, with the Library of Congress and the National Commission on Libraries and Information Science, has served as the agency to bring together a number of organizations and individuals to participate in the design and initial development of the projected bibliographic system.

In announcing the new Bibliographic Service Development Program, the Council stated that:

Fundamental to future success is the fact that projected system improvement will be built on past accomplishments, including (1) the standardized data bases generated at the Library of Congress since 1968; (2) the demonstrated success of OCLC, Inc., in supplying promptly and economically millions of catalog cards to hundreds of member libraries; (3) the skills, knowledge, and techniques acquired in the process of developing sophisticated information retrieval systems at the Library of Congress, the National Library of Medicine, OCLC, Inc., the Washington State Library, Chicago, Stanford, Toronto, Northwestern, and several other universities; (4) the efforts of the Research Libraries Group, NELINET (New England Library Information Network), SOLINET (Southeastern Library Network), and others to establish new administrative and governing mechanisms suited to cooperative undertakings; (5) the growing body of accepted standards controlling record content and format that are essential to building a durable bibliographic structure in a systematic way; and (6) an improved understanding by all those involved of the work to be done and clear evidence of a willingness to participate in a cooperative undertaking of great difficulty, yet of even greater importance.

Grants from private foundations and the National Endowment for the Humanities, totaling over $5 million, have been pledged to cover the first five years of work. The experience with this initial venture should provide guidance for the continued development and expansion of the bibliographic system. What is needed now is cooperation from other potential participants and the active involvement of scholarly societies, particularly in disciplines that have not already developed computerized bibliographic data bases. Further developmental funds will be necessary in future years as the need for additional services arises.

Furthermore, the future of new forms of publication such as on-demand will depend critically upon the quality and comprehensiveness of bibliographic coverage. Inclusion in a well-organized and accessible bibliographic system will be absolutely essential if material recorded or stored for distribution on-demand is to stand any chance of being identified and used. One of the benefits of a national periodicals center, discussed in Recommendation Two, would be the expansion of on-demand publication of materials that have a limited market; however, that potential will not be realized without the parallel development of a comprehensive bibliographic system. Thus, the potential benefits of a national bibliographic network can be magnified by the development of a periodicals center, both serving as component parts of an improved system for scholarly communication.

Recommendation Two: A national periodicals center
> We recommend the establishment of a national periodicals center and endorse the plan for its development, operation, management, and financing prepared by the Council on Library Resources.

By enhancing the capability of scholars to identify materials relevant to their research interests, an improved bibliographic system will increase the borrowing requests directed to libraries. In order to meet these requests, it will be necessary to develop more reliable and more cost-effective methods for library resource-sharing. Creation of a national periodicals center promises to meet that need for journal and other periodical publications.

Endorsed in principle by the National Commission on Libraries and Information Science, the idea of a periodicals center has been much discussed in recent years. In 1977 the Library of Congress asked the Council on Library Resources to prepare a technical development plan for the center, and that report was released in August 1978. For the center to become a reality, federal legislation authorizing its creation and financing must be enacted; such legislation will probably be introduced during the Ninety-Sixth Congress. We add our support to those who see this legislation as essential to ensuring that the nation's research libraries can disseminate the findings of research and scholarship effectively to all potential users.

The operating objectives of the center are clearly stated in the Council on Library Resources report:

1. To provide a reliable method of access to a comprehensive collection of periodical literature.

2. To reduce the overall costs of acquiring periodical material by interlibrary loan (ILL).

3. To reduce the time required to obtain requested material.

4. To assure that for any document delivered through the NPC, all required copyright fees and obligations will have been paid.

5. To act, under appropriate conditions, as a distribution agent for publishers.

6. To provide libraries with additional options as they establish their own collection development and maintenance policies.

7. To promote the development of local and regional resource sharing.

8. To contribute to the preservation of periodical material.

9. To provide a base for the development of new and imaginative publication strategies.

10. To provide a working example of a national access service that might be extended to other categories of materials.

Given the Enquiry's emphasis on effective scholarly communication, several innovative features of this plan stand out. First, the center is not presented as simply a large storehouse for journals and other periodical literature, meant to serve exclusively as the source of materials for inter-library loan. Instead, a more active role is proposed, with the center acting as a distribution agent for publishers of certain types of materials. Second, the national periodicals center will ensure that all copied material is delivered in full compliance with the copyright laws, thus relieving libraries of some of the requirements established by the CONTU (National Commission on New Technological Uses of Copyrighted Works) guidelines. Third, a price schedule will be established for each item, taking into account such factors as its copyright status, age, and the frequency with which it is requested. The fees charged will be used in part to compensate publishers for any legally required copyright fees or possible sales fees. Fourth, the existence of this facility will open new possibilities for growth of alternative forms of publication, such as on-demand or synoptic publishing. Fifth, the center will provide librarians with the option of relying on it for little-used material, rather than subscribing to the journal or relying solely on interlibrary loan. And, most important, its existence will expand access to the full range of research materials to scholars and all others who are not located at major universities.

Since there has been misunderstanding of the proposal for the national periodicals center, it needs to be stressed that the center will *not* give rise to wholesale cancellations by libraries of journal subscriptions. There is simply no substitute in the scholarly process for browsing through current journals as a stimulus to thought and further research, and librarians are as aware of that fact as are faculty members. Whether the center is created or not, however, the fact remains that financial pressures will continue to force librarians to exercise greater selectivity over journal acquisition and retention. In the absence of the center, the ability of libraries to serve the needs of scholars efficiently and effectively will steadily erode. Its existence will allow librarians to develop local collections of maximum value to users, secure in the knowledge that a reliable source exists for acquiring back issues and seldom-used items.

Recommendation Three: A national library agency
We recommend that a new organization be created to help plan and bring about the purposeful development of a national library system.

Although libraries have been growing at exponential rates in recent decades, the rapid growth in cost and volume of publications means that each library is becoming increasingly less able to satisfy the research and educational needs of its users. The linking together of library resources through a nationwide bibliographic network, and the creation of a national periodicals center, are two of the responses necessary to create a capacity greater than any individual library can offer, and both are steps toward a purposefully created national library system. Additional components of this system will need to be developed, including a coordinated approach to preservation of materials and the identification and division of responsibility for maintaining (or creating) national collections. An operating agency with the mandate and funds to encourage the development of these components of a library system is necessary if the effort is to succeed.

In advancing this recommendation, we acknowledge the important and continuing role of the Library of Congress, but also recognize the need for a separate agency able to undertake and concentrate resources on new activities required by the nation's library system. These activities, which are not fully included in the current Library of Congress mandate, are development and management of the national periodicals center, development and operation of a nationwide bibliographic system, and implementation of a preservation program for deteriorating books and other scholarly materials. The new agency would work closely with the Library of Congress—which is central to the national library system—and with the nation's research libraries and others in carrying out these new functions. Without such an agency, specifically charged with accomplishing these tasks, the chances are great that the activities will not be implemented in a timely fashion.

A national periodicals center would be the first operating program of a national library agency. The center is inseparably linked, however, to the nation's bibliographic structure, the evolving library communications network, and the complex processes of resource development and preservation.

The purposes of a national library agency should therefore include the following:

- To coordinate bibliographic control for the significant scholarly and research material of the world so that library patrons, scholars, and research personnel are not restricted in their work only to publications in their own libraries
- To facilitate the development, dissemination, and acceptance of national and international standards for bibliographic description and communications and for networking
- To ensure access, through lending or reproduction consistent with applicable laws, to published information of all kinds and formats which are needed by scholars but which their libraries are unable to acquire or retain
- To assure a program for the preservation of published information through conservation techniques and maintenance of depositories for infrequently used materials in order that the accumulated experience, knowledge, and literature of the past will not be lost.

A national library agency should be governed by a body with the responsibility and authority to establish, fund, coordinate, operate, or contract for the programs and services required to carry out the purposes of the agency, to determine operating policies, and to evaluate and review management performance. The governing body should be designed, and its membership selected, with the same sensitivity to the subject of government presence which has shaped the character of the governing boards of the National Science Foundation and the National Endowments for the Arts and Humanities. Persons nominated should be drawn from the ranks of scholars, scientists, university trustees and officers, head librarians, publishers, and public figures with demonstrated broad intellectual interests.

Of course, a national library agency would have no prescriptive authority over the activities of the nation's libraries. The agency should be limited to organizing and directing national services to augment local capabilities, and to cooperative efforts that permit individual libraries to operate more effectively and efficiently.

Recommendation Four: Controlling journal growth

We recommend that further net growth in the number of scholarly journals be discouraged—not by artificial barriers to the establishment of new journals, but by a continuing scrutiny of the usefulness and quality of existing journals as well as of those that are proposed. Librarians, university administrators, and individual scholars share the responsibility for carrying on this evaluation.

During the period when the Enquiry conducted its Survey of Scholars, more journals were being launched than were being shut down, despite the prevailing view among scholars that enough journals were already being published, and among librarians that proliferation was straining library budgets. No evidence has come to our attention that the supply of journals is inadequate to meet the needs of scholarly communication in general. In some disciplines, however, new journals may be needed, and if so, they should be started. Although some observers deplore the ease with which small journals can be started, we view this ease of entry into publishing as an advantage when not contrived for self-serving interest. It helps assure that channels of communication are kept open. But even during the recent period of journal growth there have been deaths as well as births, and we consider this turnover to be healthy. In short, no artificial barriers should be erected to block the introduction of new journals, but neither should universities or foundations provide subsidies to prop up failing journals that do not enjoy a strong reader loyalty.

Recommendation Five: Economies for small journals

We recommend that small independent journals seek production, subscription fulfillment, and other services from large established journals, university presses, learned societies, or other organizations that can offer the economies that small operations cannot obtain on their own.

Both commercial and nonprofit publishers have demonstrated that greater efficiency results when operations are large enough to be performed by a permanent professional staff effectively supported by appropriate technology. Much of the financial difficulty confronting small publishers results from their higher costs. If they are to survive, two major approaches are available, both of which are consistent with the continued independence of editorial control: (1) assignment of publishing responsibilities to a commercial publisher, a nonprofit publishing organization, or a university press, or (2) purchasing production and other services from a learned society, following the model of the American Anthropological Association and the journals it serves, or the similar arrangement envisioned by the Modern

Language Association. Either approach is workable. The essential point is that the editorial responsibility can be split off from other publishing responsibilities, simplifying the scholar's work and providing professional support for those aspects of publishing in which the scholar's expertise is limited. A third alternative is also feasible, but is probably riskier than the other two: formation of a consortium to provide production and distribution services.

Recommendation Six: Cooperation with the Copyright Clearance Center
> We recommend that all journals, libraries, and scholars cooperate with the program of the Copyright Clearance Center in order to simplify the dissemination of scholarly information and compensate copyright owners for the use of copyrighted material.

The recent far-reaching revisions of the copyright law were worked out painfully and painstakingly over several years with the full participation of representatives of authors, publishers, and libraries. Innovations, such as the Copyright Clearance Center, which were devised to help carry out the intent of the law, warrant a fair test. The copyright-clearance procedure has a dual purpose: first, to systematize and simplify the use of copyrighted material; and, second, to compensate the copyright owners for the use of the material. We think both objectives should be pursued. If the center is successful, the dissemination of scholarly information will be greatly enhanced and the creators of material will benefit as well. By offering their cooperation, journals, libraries, and scholars (many of whom will have to give up old habits of casually recopying materials for classroom use) can provide encouragement and increase the chances of the center's success.

If a national periodicals center is created, the Copyright Clearance Center will take on added importance since a sharp increase in photocopied items should occur. Publishers, scholars, and librarians will all have an important stake in the success of these two national centers.

Recommendation Seven: The market for books abroad
> We recommend a vigorous effort to promote sales of scholarly books abroad through (a) cooperative efforts and improvements in service that can be undertaken by the presses themselves, (b) the reestablishment of a government guarantee program that would make it easier to surmount currency exchange problems, import restrictions, and other impediments to international trade, and (c) foundation support to finance the start-up costs of new ventures.

If the Enquiry's estimate of foreign sales possibilities is correct, the market in other countries offers a major opportunity to scholarly publishers. Successful efforts to tap that market could recoup much of the decline in sales per title that has occurred in the 1970s. Data on foreign sales—ranging from negligible sales up to 25 percent of total sales for some presses— illustrate the potential. Major obstacles to purchases of U.S. books by foreign buyers include a lack of information about available titles, lack of uniformity in procedures for ordering, poor service, and surcharges on books sold abroad. These are all remediable problems, but since the foreign buying public is widely scattered, presses are generally not able to solve them individually. Particularly in developing countries, no press has a large enough business to mount a large promotional and distributional program. Collective efforts or tie-ins with established operations are clearly essential if the costs of better performance are to be checked. That such collective efforts can be viable has already been demonstrated. About one-third of the presses are represented in London by offices that they jointly maintain. But outside of London and Western Europe there is virtually no representation of university presses except for the handful of presses that maintain an office at the University of Hawaii to cover the Pacific, East Asia, and the Near East. One major obstacle to foreign sales cannot be handled by the presses themselves: the problems posed by the exchange of foreign currencies and import limitations. Here governmental aid, such as a program to guarantee publishers against losses resulting from fluctuation in foreign exchange rates, would be essential.

Recommendation Eight: The role of universities without presses

To broaden support for scholarly publishing, we recommend that universities without presses become active participants in the publishing process as sponsors of work produced on their campuses.

From a publishing perspective, there are two kinds of colleges and universities: those that have presses and those that do not. The publishing initiative in the United States is now concentrated in the relative handful of universities that have presses (about sixty-five), and the burden of subsidizing scholarly publication falls on these same institutions. The other 1,500 or so universities and four-year colleges neither participate in the publishing process nor help pay the cost. We believe that they could and should participate constructively in both functions. There are a number of ways in which they can do so, ranging from title subsidies to participation in a consortium (such as the University Press of New England established by Brandeis University, Clark University, Dartmouth College, the University of New Hampshire, the University of Rhode Island, and the University of Vermont).

The broadest program would be one in which 100 or 200 universities offered title subsidies annually (or every other year) of $1,000 to $3,000 each to support the publication of meritorious manuscripts produced on campus—manuscripts that otherwise would probably not be published without a subsidy either because the work was unusually costly to print or would be of interest to only a very small audience. The winner of an award would be free to offer the manuscript to any nonprofit publisher, and the final decision on publication would be made by the publisher. The publisher would agree to recognize the role of the sponsoring university by publishing on the title page a statement, such as the following: "Published in cooperation with ____ College by the ____ University Press." Smaller colleges and universities could participate in such a program on an *ad hoc* basis with smaller grants. A cooperative effort to encourage widespread participation might well be considered by a scholarly organization, such as the American Council of Learned Societies, which is especially concerned about sustaining the publication of works in the humanities. Foundation support in the form of matching grants would be useful in encouraging universities to participate.

An institution that seeks a more active role may consider establishing a series of books under its own imprint—either for a special area such as the humanities or for any manuscripts produced on its campus. The series would be published by an established press which would give appropriate recognition to the sponsoring institution. A subsidy for one or more titles a year would be sufficient to keep a series active.

A still more active role would be partnership in an established press. Small university presses should be encouraged to strengthen themselves by establishing consortia along the lines of the University Press of New England.

The purpose of this recommendation is to encourage universities and colleges to consider the full range of alternatives whereby they can join in the communication of scholarly knowledge and help strengthen the financial underpinnings of scholarly publishing. These alternatives should have special appeal to those universities that have considered establishing presses but have backed away because of the cost. Subsidizing a series of books or

individual titles would be far less costly and could gain recognition for the
university while providing assistance to individual scholars.

Recommendation Nine: A broader role for foundations
We recommend greater foundation support for scholarly communication—grants for systemwide improvements, funds to encourage collaboration among publishers, and title subsidies (particularly for the
publication of foundation-supported research that has been judged to be
meritorious).

Foundations have played an important role in the development of
scholarly publishing for a half century. Title subsidies, grants for specific
publishing projects, and grants to individual presses have been indispensable
in promoting the growth and improvement of scholarly publishing. But each
step forward has opened up new opportunities, and as this report makes
clear, there is a large agenda of publishing activities that can benefit from
foundation support.

Up to now, support has come mostly from a few major foundations and
a few middle-sized ones, which collectively account for only a tiny fraction
of the total number of foundations in the United States. In our view, a
broader participation of foundations in the support of scholarly communication—through title subsidies or financing of special projects, for example—would be highly desirable. The great majority of foundations, which
have never supported dissemination activities, should begin to consider
applications for support of publication in their fields of interest.

The large foundations—such as Rockefeller, Ford, and Andrew W.
Mellon, which have made sizable grants in the past—might well put greater
emphasis on helping to finance major projects that cut across the interests of
the various participants in the scholarly communication network. For example, if universities without presses and small foundations step in to meet the
need for title subsidies, the large foundations can turn to systemwide projects
without fear that scholars needing title subsidies will be abandoned. Candi-
dates for support include the development of a national bibliographic network and experimentation with new technologies. In such activities, matching grants by several foundations can make possible the undertaking of
large-scale programs that cannot be financed or managed by groups of
libraries or publishers alone. Federal agencies, such as the National
Endowment for the Humanities, are also logical partners in such enterprises.

Equally appropriate would be foundation grants to the scholarly presses as a group to expand their international distribution. (See Recommendation Seven.) Seed money to help finance collaborative efforts that would give small presses the benefits of larger-scale operations also should be considered.

Particular attention needs to be given by each foundation to the dissemination of the results of research that it has financed. Publication, or other forms of dissemination such as workshops, should be the culmination of most successful research projects. We believe strongly that the task of research has not been completed until the results have been made accessible to those who can make use of them.

Recommendation Ten: Collaboration in fulfillment
Scholarly presses should collaborate in the management of fulfillment centers for processing orders, warehousing, and shipping.

Unit costs of order-processing, warehousing, and shipping drop significantly as the size of these operations is increased. The economies achieved through computerization and mechanization can be very great for small presses, and even some very large ones such as Harvard and the Massachusetts Institute of Technology have found it economical to combine warehousing and shipping operations. Presses with annual sales of about $500,000 or less—which comprise nearly half of the membership of the Association of American University Presses—are generally allocating a much higher proportion of their budgets for these fulfillment costs than are the largest presses. One way to reduce these costs is to buy services from larger presses. For example, the Johns Hopkins University Press provides services to meet quite different needs of three other presses. An alternative is for several small presses to form a consortium—a more difficult solution than buying services from an established press, but one that is feasible. The workability of cooperative endeavors has been demonstrated by the successful consortia formed by scholarly presses to handle foreign sales. The payoff is not only lower costs, but better performance and better service for users.

Cost arguments are compelling, but there are other reasons, related to the main emphasis of this report, for presses to combine fulfillment operations. Libraries, wholesalers, and scholars (who buy most of their books directly from publishers) would not need to send their orders to so many places. Shipments could be consolidated, especially foreign shipments. The order-processing system in a center can be efficiently computerized not only for handling orders (based on International Standard Book Numbers) but for improving management through historical sales analysis, credit control, and so forth. In the more distant future, computerized fulfillment centers can be directly linked with libraries to provide information by wire or wireless—bibliographical information, abstracts, or even printouts. Some publishers' fulfillment centers are already linked with wholesalers in this way.

Recommendation Eleven: An office of scholarly communication
We recommend the establishment of an office of scholarly communication within the National Endowment for the Humanities for the continuing study and monitoring of the system for scholarly communication in the humanities and social sciences.

Our first ten recommendations are intended to produce evolutionary change in the system of scholarly communication to enable that system to continue serving effectively the changing needs of scholarship. We do not advance these recommendations as solutions for all problems, however, for the terrain we have attempted to cover is vast and much of it remains unexplored. We are also mindful of how our perception of the problems and their severity has changed during the Enquiry's life, and of the consequent changes in our view of sensible policy steps. For these reasons, this report should be seen not as a culminating event, but as a contribution to sustained investigation of the scholarly communication system as it continues to evolve.

Ensuring an effective communication system is clearly in the nation's interest, and our experience with the National Enquiry has convinced us of three things in this regard. First, the problems will be ever-changing, as new developments in one sector of the system change the operating conditions for the other groups. Second, the systems approach that was taken by the Enquiry is a valuable way to view the issues, for the interactions among scholars, learned societies, universities, presses, journals, libraries, and technology are many and cannot be ignored. Third, the information available on which to base judgments about emerging problems and needed improvement in the humanities is sparse or nonexistent, and it is nowhere collected and coordinated from a perspective of concern for the total communications network. For these reasons, an office of scholarly communications could perform a valuable service for the constituent enterprises that make up the system of scholarly communication, as well as for the National

Endowment for the Humanities in forming its own policies toward those constituent groups.

Among other functions, this office should monitor the births and deaths of journals, the number of new books published by discipline, submission, and acceptance rates for a sample of journals and presses, time required from acceptance to publication, and trends in library acquisitions. In addition, the office would perform special studies as problems arise. For example, many professors have expressed concern in recent years over the number of books going out of print, which restricts the range of possible college course offerings. To our knowledge, no systematic survey of this development has been made, and thus the severity of the problem is not known. The office of scholarly communication would be the logical agency to conduct such a survey.

The information collected and analyzed by this office would provide a continuing ability to assess the health of scholarly communication, serving thereby to identify emerging problems and to suggest solutions. The office would perform many of the same services for the humanities that the Division of Science Information of the National Science Foundation performs for the scientific disciplines, and would provide valuable information to the standing committee proposed in the next recommendation.

Recommendation Twelve: The intelligent use of technology

We recommend that the American Council of Learned Societies join with the Association of American University Presses and the Association of Research Libraries in establishing a standing committee composed of scholars, publishers, and librarians for continuing discussion of the nature and direction of technological change in the system of scholarly communication.

The next decade will present the scholarly community with numerous choices regarding new technologies that can be adopted in libraries and in scholarly book and journal publishing. From the vantage of scholarly communication, the potential for making unwise choices among these technologies is great, particularly if scholars are not active participants in the decision-making discussions. A continuing forum is needed to bring together scholars, librarians, publishers, and technologists for the purpose of discussing the potentials of new communication technologies, the methods and procedures required for their implementation, and their effects on the working arrangements of scholars and other users of recorded knowledge.

Drawing on our experience with the National Enquiry, we have found that a diverse group of individuals representing the several constituent groups that make up the system of scholarly communication can work together productively on problems of common concern. Thus, we have reason to believe that a similarly constituted group could work effectively in providing guidance to those who must decide on the nature and direction of technological change in libraries and in publishing. The American Council of Learned Societies, the Association of American University Presses, and the Association of Research Libraries should assume the responsibility for establishing a jointly sponsored standing committee, with members drawn from their ranks, to meet regularly for this purpose. The potential changes sketched speculatively in the Epilogue to this chapter need to be guided by the intelligence and wisdom that resides in the affected communities, not by technological and economic forces alone.

EPILOGUE: A LONGER VIEW

For as long as any of us can remember, the system of scholarly communication has worked in the following way: Scholars toiled in the library or in their studies or by doing research in the field; they wrote what they had to say; the writings were judged by their peers; some writings fell by the wayside or went back for revision, but the best were published in journals or books; the journals and books were collected and arranged in libraries where other scholars could use them. It was a cyclical flow that continually renewed itself and enriched human knowledge and understanding. It was a good system, and it worked well until recently.

The old system has run into trouble because it has not been able to accommodate the explosion of knowledge that it itself has played a part in creating. Especially after World War II the self-renewing character of the old system produced an exponential growth that began to reach the limits of the environment in which it had to live. In this kind of situation many organisms (or writings) cannot survive, and evolution takes place more rapidly. There is intense competition for survival; thus it can be said that publication is too difficult. There is also more published than the system (or the mind of a scholar) can absorb or sustain; thus it can equally be said that publication is too easy.

In addressing the problems of scholarly communication, we have stated several times that our recommendations are evolutionary, but toward what are they evolving? It will be useful at this point to look far ahead to try to see in a general way how the scholar will be working in the twenty-first century. It can be argued that the new technology of printing led directly over 300 years to the Industrial Revolution, which has lasted some 200 years to the mid-twentieth century, where we are now faced with an electronic-information revolution. It is not unreasonable to think that the next revolution will take some 25 to 50 years, although some basic changes are already taking place.

Let us imagine a scholar—an historian or a classicist or a philosopher—in an office or study, working to understand some scholarly problem. He or she will, we believe, have books and paper and pens and pencils and a typewriter, but there will be other things too. The typewriter will be part of a computer terminal. The work, as it is written, will come out as typewriting on paper, but it will also be stored in the memory of the computer. The scholar can enter revisions in the computer by giving simple instructions and can have the revised version retyped by pushing a button. If information is needed on a particular problem, the scholar can, through the typewriter, ask the computer for a bibliography, which will be typed out in response to the question, or it may flash up in video display (on a television tube) attached to the typewriter. Selecting an item of interest from the bibliography, the scholar may turn to a console in the corner of the office (or it may be down the hall where the photoduplicating machine used to be) and summon up through a national network the images of the pages that are of greatest interest. They can be read on a video screen, and if they are needed for further study, the scholar can push a button and get a printout of the pages required. If many pages are needed, perhaps a whole book, a telephone call to the university library will bring a photoduplicate of the microfiche of the book that is stored there—or the university library can get the microform from one in a network of sources. The scholar may go to the library to browse among the books (there will still be books) and microforms (with greatly improved microform readers), but the library has also assumed a major function as an electronic link between scholars on the campus and a national or even international network of information centers where writing is stored in many different forms—microforms, tapes, disks, electronic storage in computers, and even in books and journals.

In short, tremendous resources will be easily available. The scholar will not have to spend so much time digging in libraries, traveling, and being frustrated because the book that is wanted is not there, or will take three weeks to acquire. More time can be spent thinking and writing—and teaching. The scholar's essential work is still done with the mind; that will be just as difficult as ever—perhaps more difficult because there will be more possibilities and more information.

When the work is finished as a piece of writing, it must meet the test (as now) of criticism from other scholars. As now, the scholar must seek one of a number of channels into the communication system if the work is to be read by other scholars and win recognition. The scholar may submit it to any one of a number of publishers, including both commercial and university publishers, or to the editorial board of a scholarly society, or to a research institute—to some recognized validating agency—before it is entered into the communication system. If the work falls below a reasonable standard of quality, it will be rejected. Or, we would hope, it would pass muster, at which point the publisher would give it its imprint and enter it into the system.

We have sketched the output of the system, but what is the system like? How does one enter it? That is the decision of the publisher, and to some extent, it will be determined by the author's choice of a publisher, since publishers will be more specialized than today, both by subject and by mode. There will be many publishers making independent evaluations on the basis of expert advice; we will not have a monolithic system controlled at a single point of entry. A number of publishers will still issue printed books, although the technology of producing them will be different. Many of these will be works of scholarship that are expected to reach a wide range of scholars and students or to go also in considerable numbers to the general public.

We want here to distinguish between books that are *read* and those that are *used*. A scholar uses many books and other materials, frequently consulting only parts of books or articles, or skimming them, or looking up a few items in the index. Books that are mainly to be used in this way can be satisfactory in microform, especially when better projectors are available. But there are many scholarly books, especially in the humanities, that are read at length, and reread, and pondered. A scholar wants to own such books, which can be underlined or marginally annotated or outlined or indexed in the endpapers. Books of this kind, integrating much study and hard thinking over long years, will be needed in traditional form. This fact applies not only to the great books of our intellectual heritage but to a substantial number of new books every year, books that draw on the past to help us understand the human condition today. Publishers, with the help of scholars, will have to decide which books to issue in traditional form and which in other forms. Probably many will be issued in several ways.

The traditional book is an extraordinarily convenient and inexpensive artifact (even at today's prices); we do not believe it will become obsolete. But many works of specialized scholarship will in the future be entered into the system in other ways, for more efficient access and storage—in microform or on tapes or disks, to be retrieved at computer terminals on video displays or by printouts on demand. The entire bibliography will be computer-controlled. Technology will provide printouts much more like printed books than they are today, with readable typefaces and attractive paper so that aesthetic standards can be reasserted.

We want to emphasize that aesthetic considerations are not to be ignored. The humanities are concerned with human values, including the value of beauty, and aesthetics are part of the very substance of the humanities. An ugly book of art history or literary criticism or musicology is a contradiction in terms. If we care about the subjects that make up the humanities, we care about aesthetics. Technologists must understand that humanistic scholarship is not merely information or data and that its human character must somehow be transmitted through the medium of the machine.

Who pays? Once the system exists, the publisher must pay to enter writings into it. The cost will probably not be large, at least in the "manufacturing" category of expense, because it can be entered with the magnetic tapes from the author's terminal, or with an optical character recognition (OCR) scanning the author's typescript. Editing on typescript or on video display can be done before the manuscript is entered. Or the tape can be run through a computer-typesetting device to emerge as a book that can be put in microform or printed. The computer keeps track of uses of the images, for which the library or the user must pay—to recompense both publisher and author and to pay for the system. The publisher will still have selection, design, and promotion functions, but he will be selling images, not physical copies.

All the technology for this scenario exists now. All the procedures described are now in practical use—some are even in common use—typewriter and video terminals for input–output and editing of hard copy, OCR, computer searches, networking, full-size microform printouts, remote facsimile, and so forth. Two things keep the system as described from existing today, cost and organization. This is clearly shown in the operation of the Bell Laboratories Library System where some twenty-two libraries from

New Jersey to Colorado operate in a network for the purpose of supporting Bell Laboratories research. Organization is not a problem because the top management of Bell Labs can decree and specify a system to support the whole; the interests of the groups within the system are subordinated. Cost is a factor only in that the top management, with enormous financial resources and access to the highest technology, looks at the total output of knowledge in relation to its total cost. Again, the costs and incomes of the sectors within the system are subordinated. We do not think the Bell Labs Library System can be a model for an evolving system of scholarly communication—it is too monolithic and too specialized—but much can be learned from it. Among other things, we can learn that the individual groups in the public system will have to change their functions as new technologies are adopted for economic reasons. The boundaries between scholar-authors and publishers and the book trade (especially library wholesalers) and libraries and scholar-readers will shift and blur. New librarylike services will be offered by publishers and wholesalers, scholars will enter materials directly into libraries, libraries will perform publisherlike or bookstorelike functions.

These changes should not be resisted, but we must expect rearguard actions from those who feel threatened by change. Patience will be required; new systems will not be introduced without a few gremlins that will have to be exorcised. Forward-looking and ingenious entrepreneurs will seize on changes to advance and exploit them, which will probably be beneficial. We will continue to have a mixed public and private system with some centralized functions (especially bibliographic) and with many points of entry and of output.

A national and ultimately international information system, connected by wire or wireless, working through a network of libraries and national resource centers, can and will eventually be established. It will be a difficult accomplishment, but it will be done because of the need to extend access to recorded information and because cost factors will require it as the cost of labor keeps rising and the cost of electronics keeps dropping. The system that is eventually evolved will perhaps not look very much like what we have described; no doubt it will be better. The problems in establishing such a system are not mainly technical; they are organizational and behavioral. In a short-term sense, they are also economic because the starting costs will be great; large investments of capital will be needed. But in the long term the driving force for change will be economic because the present system is reaching a state of saturation that is increasingly unworkable and costly.

The challenge to the National Enquiry has been to recommend changes in the present system of scholarly communication—changes that are practical and evolutionary and which can be motivated—that will move us from the present toward the establishment of a new national and even international system.

CHAPTER 2

Scholarly Journals

The journal is an efficient, flexible, and effective method of communi-cation, and it plays an essential role in the dissemination of scholarly research. Even in the humanities, where the book continues to be dominant in the number of pages printed and read, the typical scholar follows four or five journals regularly.

Despite its merits, however, the journal is often a troublesome link in the communications network, and scholars give it mixed reviews. As readers they generally express themselves satisfied, but as authors they report that getting published is often a frustrating experience. Editors find the manager-ial and financial burdens onerous. Librarians, overwhelmed in recent years by the proliferation of new journals and by sharply rising costs that have far exceeded the rate of inflation (as well as the growth in their own budgets), have sounded a call for reform.

Three issues are the focus of discussion in this chapter: First, how well do journals serve the communication needs of scholars? Second, how can the management and financing of journals be improved? Third, how realistic are various proposed alternatives or supplements to journals? These discussions are introduced by the following brief survey of the journal industry and its growth in recent years.

NUMBER AND GROWTH OF JOURNALS

A conservative estimate of the number of scholarly journals published in the United States during the late 1970s is about 2,700. Bernard M. Fry and Herbert S. White estimated the number at 2,459 in 1973,[1] and since that time the number has been increasing at an average rate of 2 or 3 percent a year,

This chapter draws on a paper prepared for the Enquiry by Nazir Bhagat.

1. Bernard M. Fry and Herbert S. White, *Publishers and Libraries: A Study of Scholarly and Research Journals* (Lexington, Mass., Lexington Books, 1976). The Fry and White sample of about 2,500 was developed by excluding seventeen categories of periodicals—such as newsletters, trade journals, and government publications—as shown in Exhibit 2.1.

Exhibit 2.1. Classification of serials, periodicals, and journals. From Fritz Machlup, Kenneth W. Leeson, and associates, *Information Through the Printed Word: The Dissemination of Scholarly, Scientific and Intellectual Knowledge* (New York, New York University, March 1978) processed.

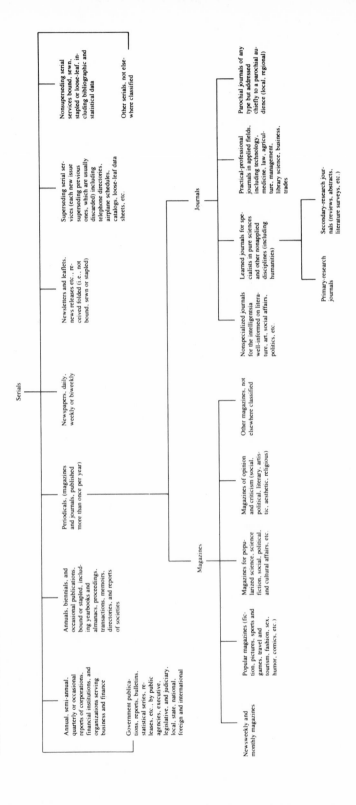

judging from subsequent editions of *Ulrich's International Periodicals Directory*. About half the journals counted by Fry and White are in the humanities and the social sciences and the remainder are in the sciences and technology.

But these figures must be viewed as approximations. There are no universally applied, unambiguous criteria for drawing the line between scholarly journals, on the one hand, and trade and professional journals on the other—between journals and other periodicals—and between periodicals and serials in general.

The problems of classification are illustrated by Exhibit 2.1, which shows scholarly journals in the constellation of serials.[2] As the diagram indicates, *serials* is a broad term. There are perhaps 100,000 serials issued annually in the world—including 60,000 periodicals, listed in *Ulrich's Directory for 1977–78*, plus 32,500 serials listed in the companion volume, *Irregular Serials and Annuals: An International Directory*.[3]

Scholarly journals comprise a narrow category. Excluded are a variety of other scholarly publications—bibliographies, digests, abstracts, collections of book reviews, literary magazines, or newsletters reporting original research. Also excluded is the broader category of periodicals, including general magazines and newspapers, which, though they may print some scholarly material, are intended for general readership. Periodicals, in turn, are part of a still broader category—serials—which includes yearbooks, monographs, and other publications that appear at regular or irregular intervals. The focus of this chapter is on a small fraction of this output, several hundred journals in the humanities and humanistic social sciences (anthropology, history, and some areas in sociology in some tabulations).

Persisting problems in the controlling of serials—which have been troubling to librarians and researchers—led the Library of Congress and participating research libraries to develop the CONSER project (an acronym for Conversion of Serials), a machine-readable file of serials originally established by the Council on Library Resources. The purpose of this project

2. Fritz Machlup, Kenneth W. Leeson, and associates, *Information Through the Printed Word: The Dissemination of Scholarly, Scientific and Intellectual Knowledge* (New York, New York University, March 15, 1978). Preliminary report of a study carried out under grants from the National Science Foundation and the National Endowment for the Humanities. Subsequently published in three volumes by Praeger Publishers, Inc. (New York, 1978).
3. *Ulrich's International Periodicals Directory, Seventeenth Edition, 1977–1978* (Bowker, 1977); *Irregular Serials and Annuals: An International Directory* (Bowker, 1977).

Table 2.1. Growth in Humanistic Journals, 1960–75

| | Number | | Percentage change |
	1960	1975	1960–75
Classics	8	12	50
English and American literature	39	114	192
History	62	100	61
Philosophy	39	91	113
Total	148	317	114

Sources: Ulrich's International Periodicals Directory and the American Philosophical Association. (Because of differences in definition, figures in the Enquiry study, MLA reports, King, and Fry and White are not comparable, but all the studies show the same trends.)

was to build an on-line catalog of serials and to increase the use of International Standard Serial Numbers, which provide a unique numerical identifier for each serial. The file seeks to provide up-to-date information on size, frequency, circulation, price, and subject classification. Thus, it could facilitate serial selection by libraries as well as provide a better statistical base for assessing coverage of fields, and the growth and decline in the number of publications.

Whether the number of scholarly journals now being published is about right, too large, or too small—and whether some fields are better served than others—cannot be readily inferred from the studies that have been made. The figures on births and cessations suggest that there is a continual testing and adaptation, encouraging evidence of vitality. Scholars differ, depending on their perspective as author or reader. Librarians are apt to think there may be too many journals. And the market test is not very satisfactory because journal prices vary widely from costs—either because of direct and indirect subsidies, or because uniqueness enables publishers of some journals to set prices far in excess of cost. Still, the market is often the decisive influence: the scholarly network publishes the number of journals it can afford to support and this may be greater or smaller than some observers would prefer.

What is measurable, however, is growth in selected areas, and there is no doubt that there has been an explosion in the number of journals. As early as 1961, when the Modern Language Association (MLA) published the third of a series of reports on scholarly journals, the increase in the number of journals was already a matter of concern. In the fifth report of the series, Pell reported an increase from 166 journals in 1965 to 216 in 1971.[4] During the fifteen-year period from 1960 to 1975, according to King, the number of scientific and technical journals published in the United States, excluding bulletins and newsletters, increased by 50 percent from 2,800 to 4,200—an average growth rate of 3 percent annually.[5] No figures for the number of scholarly journals in the humanities are provided in that report, but an Enquiry study of scholarly journals in four humanistic disciplines revealed an even more rapid growth rate over the same period.[6] In these areas the total number of journals doubled, as shown in table 2.1.

Of the 317 journals on the market in 1975 in these disciplines, two out of three were first published between 1967 and 1972. This boom of new journals in the humanities coincided with sharp increases in the number of journals in the social sciences and in all scholarly journals. The growth in the number of journals, in turn, reflected increases in the number of faculty and graduate students. By 1973, however, the proliferation of journals in humanistic disciplines and in the humanistic social sciences began to slacken. A different selection of scholarly journals chosen by the Enquiry from six disciplines in the humanities and social sciences suggests a slowing down in average growth rates in these fields from 1973 to 1975.

A compilation by the Enquiry of the births and cessations of journals in 1975 by various disciplines shows considerable variation from discipline to discipline.[7] Professional disciplines such as medical sciences, law, economics, and library science all show substantial activity (births and cessations) and vigorous growth; forty-six new medical science journals were started and twenty-two ceased publication in 1975. Journals in applied science and technology showed high activity but no growth, and education journals had high activity and moderate growth. This activity is largely attributable to the commercial sponsorship of many journals in those fields.

4. William Pell, "Facts of Scholarly Publishing," *PMLA* (September 1973). This excellent article discusses circulation, advertising status, procedures for handling manuscripts, and financial problems. It provides a guide to the editorial preferences of the journals that were surveyed, and it also presents the results of a survey of university presses.

5. D. W. King and others, *Statistical Indicators of Scientific and Technical Communication 1960–1980*, vol. 1, prepared for the National Science Foundation (Rockville, Md., King Research, Inc., 1976).

6. Robert N. Hohwald, "A Morphology of Scholarly Journals," study for the National Enquiry.

7. Ibid.

In the humanities, English and American literature experienced substantial growth and activity similar to that seen for scientific journals. Music and philosophy experienced a moderate net growth of two to three journals per year, but there was very little change in most of the other disciplines.

Since the boom in the establishment of new journals occurred during the period of most rapid rise in university graduate enrollment and faculty and the expansion of federal funds for library purchases, it seems reasonable to expect the growth rate in the number of journals to fall in response to the leveling of enrollment and the retrenchment in spending for higher education, including libraries. New journals will, of course, continue to be founded to reflect changes in academic enrollment among disciplines, the vitality of research among disciplines, and individual initiative. We view the ease of entry into publishing as an advantage. It helps assure that channels of communication are kept open. But at the same time, journals that fail to maintain their readership should not be kept alive by subsidies but should cease publication or merge with journals with related interests. Libraries can play an important role by conducting user studies that will help identify journals that are rarely read or seldom requested for interlibrary loan. University administrators should review carefully proposals for additional journal subsidies. As indicated below, we believe that a conscious effort should be made to check the growth in the number of journals.

Recommendation 2.1.   Controlling journal growth
We recommend that further net growth in the number of scholarly journals be discouraged—not by artificial barriers to the establishment of new journals, but by a continuing scrutiny of the usefulness and quality of existing journals as well as of those that are proposed. Librarians, university administrators, and individual scholars share the responsibility for carrying on this evaluation.

THE READER'S PERSPECTIVE

A central concern of the Enquiry is whether journals are effective and efficient in disseminating research results and ideas. How do readers obtain access to journals? What are their reading habits? How do they perceive the effects of the new technologies that have been introduced in recent years or that are likely to emerge in the near future?

The following discussion reflects the finding of the Enquiry's two-part Survey of Scholars conducted in 1977.[8] One questionnaire sought to explore the habits and opinions of a sample of scholars in their role as readers. A companion questionnaire sought the views of another sample of scholars in their role as authors. Responses to each questionnaire totaled about 2,000, and they came from scholars in seven disciplines—anthropology, classics, English, history, philosophy, Romance languages, and sociology—which are loosely characterized in this report as the humanities and humanistic social sciences. The results were tabulated by discipline, by professional rank, and by the reputation of the institutions (which were classified in five tiers from most to least prestigious). Some reference is also made to the Enquiry's report of Interviews with Scholars in four humanistic disciplines, which was also conducted in 1977.[9]

What the survey shows is that scholars are very active readers who are generally satisfied with their access to publications and with the usefulness of them. Opinions and reading habits vary by discipline, institution, age, rank, teaching load, and research interests, but a number of generalizations are warranted.

JOURNALS READ AND BOUGHT. The average scholar scans seven journals, follows four or five regularly, and reads three to five articles a week. Although most of these journals are available in a campus library, the average scholar subscribes to three, two of which come as part of membership dues in a learned society.

The total amount spent on journals, membership dues and reprints averages $65 a year for humanists and $100 a year for sociologists and anthropologists. Humanists are somewhat sensitive to the price of journals to which they subscribe. Among respondents who had cancelled a journal

8. National Enquiry Survey of Scholars. Janet D. Griffith, "The Survey of Scholars: Relationships Between the Scholars and Other Estates," (Research Triangle Park, N.C., Research Triangle Institute, Center for Population and Urban–Rural Studies, 1978). The survey was planned and conducted by the Enquiry staff and analyzed and summarized by Dr. Griffith. The sample of 8,000 scholars was drawn from seven humanistic disciplines. Half the sample received an author's questionnaire and half a reader's questionnaire. The response to each was just under 50 percent—1,933 for the author questionnaire and 1,940 for the reader questionnaire. The sample provided good representation across disciplines and across five tiers of institutions (from Tier I, highly selective universities, to Tier V, less-selective four-year colleges), but it slightly overrepresented senior and highly productive scholars.

9. Jean Rafsnider, "Interviews with Scholars at Three Universities," National Enquiry.

subscription in the preceding two years, 30 percent cited an increase in price as the principal reason. Other reasons mentioned were change in research interests (24 percent) and decline in journal quality (10 percent). On the other hand, the number of reported subscription cancellations was balanced by new subscriptions. The number of individual subscriptions per scholar has not changed in recent years.

Faculty at large research universities subscribe to more journals than do scholars at other schools in spite of their access to a larger library.

READING HABITS.   Most scholars say they spend ten to twelve hours a week reading books and journals; one of four spends sixteen hours or more. Of the disciplines surveyed, historians read more than the average, and teachers of English and Romance languages less. Forty percent of the respondents indicated that the number of articles they had read has increased in the last few years, while 20 percent noted a decline. (The increase in reading was slightly more pronounced at less-prestigious institutions and also among historians and social scientists.)

Most scholars surveyed (71 percent) indicated that the last journal article they had read was from a journal to which they subscribed, and 19 percent indicated that they had acquired the article through the library. Thus, scholars rely largely on personal subscriptions for current reading in their discipline or subdiscipline. Reprints are relatively unimportant.

A study of journal readership in economics by Stephen Kagann and Kenneth W. Leeson bears out major findings of the Enquiry's Scholarly Survey.[10] As readers, economists are generally satisfied with their leading journals. Three out of four respondents called the journals either excellent or good in quality. Where they expressed dissatisfaction, they were often criticizing the direction in which research is going rather than the quality of the journal. Half the readers of the *American Economic Review,* which goes to all members of the American Economic Association, considered it too technical. Other journals, considered to be equally as technical, however, did not elicit complaints from their readers, doubtless because subscribers were self-selected rather than captive. Dissatisfaction with the *Review* reflects the wide range of interests of association members rather than any shortcomings of the *Review* itself.

10. Stephen Kagann and Kenneth W. Leeson, "Major Journals in Economics: A User Study," *Journal of Economic Literature* (September 1978).

LIBRARY USE.   The average humanist scholar conducts four or five literature searches in the library per year, but rarely uses the services of reference librarians, preferring to browse through journals in the library and to photocopy articles for future use. Speed is seldom a critical concern. Most respondents (70 percent) believe that significant literature is brought to their attention rapidly enough. Most scholars find specialized bibliographies very useful even if they are one to three years behind publicatior. (The widely used *MLA International Bibliography,* however, has substantially reduced the lag in publication. The bibliography covering 1977 was published in September 1978.) The respondents are also satisfied with interlibrary loan systems, indicating that a delay of three weeks is tolerable, provided the item arrives.

Most scholars (88 percent) said that the last article they read was published during the preceding two years. Humanists primarily read current literature to keep abreast of their field and to select research topics, but for research and writing they refer to older or archival literature, for which they depend heavily upon libraries. Whereas 74 percent of the references cited by scientists or social scientists may come from their personal collection of publications, for humanists the corresponding figure is only 36 percent. This is so, not because humanists have a smaller personal library, but because they cite more references and their needs are more diverse than those of scientists. Indeed, the same study reported that whereas less than 2 percent of the references cited by scientists and social scientists was to literature not available in the scholar's personal collection or in the local libraries, for humanists the corresponding percentage was 24 percent.

CITATION PRACTICES.   Citation studies done by the Enquiry suggest that humanists rely more on books than on journal articles for their research.[11] The number of citation references per article has increased by about 50 percent in the last ten years, and the median life of the citation references is getting somewhat shorter. One plausible inference from this expansion of references is that bibliographic tools and access to literature have been improving over the years.

Citation references in journal articles are preponderantly to other publications within the field. Nearly all citation references made in classical

11. Robert N. Hohwald, "Citations in Scholarly Journals in the Humanities and Social Sciences," study for the National Enquiry.

studies journals are to journals in classics. Corresponding figures for the other disciplines are English, 84 percent; philosophy, 82 percent; sociology, 74 percent; and history, 68 percent. These findings are consistent with statements from a majority of scholars in the personal interview study, that they usually read only the journals in their discipline. Scholars who are interdisciplinary usually read journals in only two disciplines, and few scholars read journals in more than two disciplines on a regular basis.

As yet we know little about how scholars select or define the scope of what they read. For research purposes, scholars rely on specialized bibliographies and on library collections. In the future they will have access to more on-demand services and bibliographic indices to search for and select articles to acquire (without the benefit of browsing through the text). How useful they will prove to be is uncertain, but rapid progress is being made in developing the bibliographic systems. For example, the 1977 MLA Bibliography became available in November 1978 for online searching on the Lockheed DIALOG system.

THE AUTHOR'S ASSESSMENT

It is hardly surprising that authors are less satisfied with the scholarly journal system than are readers and researchers. Even a highly efficient and fair system would cause authors considerable frustration, for publication is a long, step-by-step process in which refereeing and production, in particular, are time consuming under the best of schedules. Rejections are painful, and only a small proportion of authors escape the experience. The comments of critics and editors are a frequent source of irritation. More important, a great deal often hinges on the acceptance of an article. Whereas gaining access to reading and research materials is a weekly, if not daily, practice for the average scholar, publishing is a rare occurrence that has special significance for the author's sense of achievement and for salary increases, promotion, and tenure.

Nonetheless, the complaints of authors about pressures to publish, fairness of peer reviews, and delays in publication elicited by the Survey of Scholars, suggest that the level of dissatisfaction is higher than it needs to be, and that remedial steps are both desirable and possible. Since nearly nine out of ten respondents have published at least one article, they are familiar with difficulties of getting into print.

PRESSURES TO PUBLISH. Most academics, including 70 percent of the senior scholars responding to the Enquiry's survey, report they have felt institutional pressures to publish and believe that their positions and prestige are dependent on publishing. Moreover, as the Enquiry's survey reveals, the pressures to publish have increased in the 1970s in part because of the rise in academic unemployment and competition for advancement. They are being felt even at the less prestigious four-year colleges and, not surprisingly, have led to an increase in article writing.

While many scholars would welcome less pressure to publish, approximately half of those responding to our survey indicated that incentives to publish are desirable or beneficial to scholarship. Thus, what is implied by their responses is not an exclusion of scholarly publication from the academic evaluation process, but rather a more sensible evaluation than one that appears to be based on the number of publications or the prestige of the journal in which an article appears. Even if institutions do not employ such a simplistic measure or do not use the publications record as the sole criterion in making tenure decisions, many faculty members believe that the number of publications is frequently the criterion and that the articles or books themselves are not carefully read. It is this belief that helps account for their resentment of pressures to publish.

One way to combat the impression that numbers are decisive would be to evaluate only a limited number of the scholar's most significant works, with little credit given for publications beyond a certain number. But the underlying problem of the best way to evaluate scholarly attainment is much broader than the issue of scholarly communication, and alternatives such as the possibility mentioned above need to be considered in a broader context.

REFEREEING. Journals have a responsibility not only to select the good and reject the bad, but also to maintain or raise the quality of what is published. The refereeing system is intended to play this essential role in the scholarly communication process, serving to screen and to classify scholarly knowledge.

It seems to be working satisfactorily, though complaints have been made by young faculty that refereeing takes too long and that it is unfair. They would like to see more "openness," fuller critiques, speedier responses, anonymous submissions, and grievance boards to handle complaints. Senior scholars, on the other hand, put greater stress on maintaining the quality of what is being published. Some efforts have been made to assess bias, but they have produced no conclusive evidence.

Some editors suggest that biases in referee judgments are often attributable to differences in research style and schools of thought rather than to personal factors. Elimination of such differences in point of view among referees is neither possible nor necessarily desirable. It has been argued that if biases are ideological rather than personal the case for "anonymous submissions" (concealing the author's identity from the referees) may be debatable. Nonetheless, anonymous refereeing may be desirable if it serves only to reassure young scholars about the fairness of the refereeing process. The credibility of the process is of great importance.

Lack of agreement among referees presents a special problem for editors and affects the overall quality of published literature. In cases of disagreement, editors usually seek another review or decide the issue themselves. The routine solicitation of more opinions, however, puts an additional strain on the peer review system, sometimes to no avail.

A simple procedure to resolve disagreements and improve the quality of decision making has been tested by a number of journals. The editor requests each referee to reassess the manuscript in light of the comments of the other reviewer, which are forwarded without revealing the identity of one reviewer to another. The editor then makes the decision. This procedure has been found very useful in a variety of situations requiring group assessments.

REJECTION RATES.   Data from our Survey of Scholars indicate that 56 percent of the respondents have written an article that remains unpublished. This figure may reflect response biases, such as the reluctance of scholars to acknowledge failure or persistence in resubmitting manuscripts that have been repeatedly rejected. If valid, the figure is informative, but it falls short of answering the crucial question, Does meritorious and useful work go unpublished?

While data on manuscript submissions obtained from the Survey of Scholars may need further analysis and corroboration, they suggest the following: (1) there is great variation in the number of submissions that manuscripts undergo before being published, and (2) a published article, before its acceptance by a journal, is subject to an average of only 1.5 submissions. This implies that a high proportion of published articles are accepted on first submission and that articles which eventually are shelved have been considered several times and have probably been given a fair opportunity.

In general, the number of journals is viewed as adequate. Indeed, scholars seem as much concerned or more concerned about the threat to the integrity and quality of scholarly publishing that is posed by a continuing proliferation of journals. Some are concerned, too, about the possibility that an increased flow of articles of questionable merit will make literature searches more difficult in the future. In short, the scholar is well aware of the tradeoff between the risk of permitting undue barriers to the publication of meritorious work and the deterioration of quality.

This concern about quality is reflected in attitudes toward the selection of a journal for submission of a manuscript. Of six factors affecting this choice, the reputation of the journal was considered most important by a wide margin. Likelihood of acceptance ranked a weak second, speed of acceptance next, and size of readership as unimportant. Among assistant professors the probability of acceptance was rated as important, though not more important than the journal's reputation.

DELAYS IN PUBLICATION. In the humanistic disciplines speed is less important than in the sciences. Nevertheless, delays in the publication process, at the peer review and production stages, are a source of annoyance to scholars, though there is no evidence that the delays are getting worse.

Among suggestions for change in the publications process, four were mentioned most frequently in our Survey of Scholars. Ranked in order they are (1) speedier decision on manuscripts submitted to journals; (2) more complete critiques and reasons for rejection; (3) speedier publication after acceptance; and (4) less pressure to publish.

But although the Enquiry's survey confirms the wish of scholars to receive quicker decisions on acceptance or rejection, it does not point to a process for achieving this result. We have no data to indicate the extent to which delays are attributable to inefficiencies in the review process. Nor do we know how much is attributable to other demands on the editor's time or to delays by reviewers in completing their reviews. That is, we can document the findings that scholars consider the process too slow, but not the solution. Beyond exhortations, there is not much more that this study can do. Each editor who does not already do so needs to establish a system that assures (1) immediate notification of authors that a manuscript has been received, (2) rapid selection of referees, (3) prompt reminders when reviews are overdue, and (4) prompt notification of the author as soon as a decision is made. Referees need to be encouraged to give reasonable priority to manuscripts. At a minimum they should indicate a target date for completing the review and stick to it. What is required of them is not a substantial increase in effort, but rather greater discipline in the use of time, and what we suggest here is no more than what the best-run journals provide.

The related issue of providing more complete critiques and reasons for rejection is more difficult to respond to. It could add substantially to the burden on referees, who are already hard pressed. Whether the journals can assume greater responsibility for evaluation is dubious, though the imposition of submission fees might make it feasible. However, for the kind of critiques that seem to be desired, authors should depend more on their colleagues. Our recommendation deals only with the issue of delay.

Recommendation 2.2.   The manuscript review process
    We recommend that editors and editorial boards take steps to speed up the manuscript review process.

Frequently it takes as long after acceptance to get a journal article published as a scholarly book—about a year. Longer waits of two or three years are more frequent for journal authors than book authors. Sometimes the delay in publication of journal articles is attributable to the understandable conservatism of editors who want to make sure that they have insurance against a temporary decline in the number and quality of manuscripts or delays in refereeing. Some express a preference for a backlog of up to a year. We believe that so large a backlog is unnecessary, given the heavy flow of manuscript submissions. Where a heavy backlog of a year and a half or two years exists, we urge that editors consider printing larger issues or produce a special issue to eliminate it. Foundations can help encourage this effort by offering a modest subsidy to journals willing to publish a special issue, provided that the editor gives assurances that once the backlog is reduced a faster schedule will be maintained. Where delays are the result of inadequate resources or poor management, editorial boards or a committee representing a sponsoring association should intervene to improve the journal's performance.

Pending substantial improvement in the speed of the publication process, editors might help meet the criticisms of authors by printing in each issue the list of articles that have been accepted since the preceding issue. This step would give the author some immediate recognition and would alert readers to the existence of the article. Those especially interested in an article for their own research purposes could write to the author for a copy of the manuscript. A good deal of such informal communication already goes on, as will be discussed in chapter 3, but since it is not possible for authors to know all of those who might be interested in their work, public announcement of accepted articles would be very helpful. In short, if the publishing process cannot be speeded up, at least the communication process can be improved.

Recommendation 2.3. Delays in publication
We recommend that editors speed up the production process and take steps to reduce backlogs.

A promising way to reduce backlogs and prevent them from building up in the future is to emulate the change initiated by the *Journal of Modern History* in 1976. This quarterly now publishes three or four articles in synoptic form in each issue after they have been refereed and accepted. The articles carry the imprimatur of the journal and are available in full text from University Microfilms in hard copy or microform and also on an annual subscription basis.

SCHOLARS AS EDITORS

A random gathering of editors from the publishing world would bring together people performing quite different tasks: copy editors who labor to bring clarity, accuracy, and consistency to the manuscripts, acquisition editors who search for manuscripts, managing editors who supervise the work flow, editors-in-chief who decide what to publish or who direct large collaborative enterprises such as encyclopedias, and so on. *Editor* is a term that covers a range of occupations requiring different skills. In small organizations, however, the editor as generalist still survives, doing a little of every editorial task—in addition to a variety of other publishing chores ranging from promotion to paying the bills.

Most scholarly journals are such small operations, and most of the editors responding to the Enquiry's Survey of Editors indicated that they are personally responsible for soliciting articles, screening manuscripts, selecting referees, corresponding with authors, and copy editing—all of this while carrying on customary teaching and research activities. Editors of small literature journals generally handle production, circulation, and business tasks that in philosophy and social science journals are more frequently handled by salaried staffs.

On the other hand, the most widely circulated journals, which are generally affiliated with major learned societies, are published by large staffs with responsibilities shared among scholars, professional copy editors and production editors, promotion and advertising personnel, business managers, and so on. Many of the problems troubling editors of small journals are not problems for large journals.

The Enquiry's questionnaire was sent to a sample of 140 editors and was answered by 45 percent of them. Of the respondents, 63 percent were affiliated with journals owned by universities, or college or university departments, 20 percent with learned societies or associations, and the rest evenly divided between journals owned by individuals and those owned by university presses and foundations. Circulation of the respondents' publications ranged from 500 to 5,000—with a median of 885 in philosophy, 1,250 in literature, and 1,700 in sociology. Generalizations based on this diversity of size and disciplines blur important differences among journals and among editors, but they can be informative nonetheless on some issues.

Like scholarly readers and authors, scholars as editors have their share of worries and complaints. To begin with, they are concerned about the glut of manuscripts that afflict so many of them, and the insufficiency of subscriptions. Such concerns seem to vary by discipline (though differences in size or other factors may be at work, too). In the following tabulation, the problems cited in responses to the Enquiry's survey are ranked by importance:

	First	Second	Third
Philosophy	Too few subscriptions	Loss of subsidies; too many manuscripts	Poor quality of manuscripts
Literature	Too many manuscripts	Too few subscriptions	Large backlog; loss of subsidies
Sociology	Rising costs	Too few subscriptions	Too few quality manuscripts

Survey respondents report that the number of manuscripts submitted over the 1970–76 period increased by about 50 percent in literature, and by about 30 percent in philosophy. Over the same period literature journals increased the number of articles published by 44 percent, whereas in philosophy the increase was 11 percent.

The full cost of publishing independent journals is difficult to estimate, though it generally exceeds the income from subscriptions. Journals are able to survive because they receive subsidies from sponsors and free services from editors, referees, and others. Most of them receive free rent or storage space, free secretarial service and help from work-study students or volunteers. Half the literature editors and two-thirds of the sociology editors responding to the survey say they receive released time.

Discussions appearing in *Editors' News,* a publication issued occasionally since 1976 by the Conference of Editors of Learned Journals, sheds additional light on the views of scholar–editors and their efforts to cooperate in coping with their difficulties. Editors representing about 250 journals in the humanities are members of the conference, organized in the mid-1950s.[12]

A major complaint is that pressures to publish are largely responsible for the proliferation of manuscripts that has occurred—especially poor manuscripts written without much understanding of what makes a paper publishable and submitted without awareness of the editorial policies of different journals. As the president of the conference put it, "While editors search for manuscripts, to enhance the disciplines they serve, to enlighten the audiences they address, they have become certification tools, inundated with essays written primarily to provide credentials. . . ."[13] It has also been suggested that submissions of poor-quality manuscripts have been encouraged by the common practice of including in résumés articles that are "under consideration" in addition to published work. Because of the time required to get work reviewed and accepted, this practice is not unreasonable. But it also invites misuse by unsuccessful authors who keep submitting rejected articles to different journals, though they have no expectation of acceptance. They merely wish to be able to list work "under consideration," as evidence of their productivity. Whether this conjecture points to a major cause of proliferation is not clear since quantitative evidence is lacking.

Editors would prefer to see either less emphasis on publication as a criterion for academic advancement or, if this change is not made, they think they merit more support from the university community for providing a certification function that properly should be performed by the faculty.

Editors think, too, that authors ought to be able to prepare better manuscripts and use better judgment in deciding where to send them. The conference of editors has sponsored workshops on these problems at several annual meetings in an effort to be helpful. Their complaint is the counterpart to the complaint of authors who responded to the Enquiry questionnaire by

12. Personal communication from Marilyn Gaull, president of the conference. This section is based primarily on her comments and on articles appearing in *Editors' News* (Spring 1978).

13. Marilyn Gaull, "President's Report," *Editors' News* (Spring 1978) p. 3.

calling for help on precisely these issues. Given this common recognition of a problem by authors and editors, support from learned societies or foundations to conduct such workshops certainly appears worth consideration. Such workshops might also deal with some of the authors' criticisms of journals which editors think are unwarranted.

In *Editors' News* it is also pointed out that editors are burdened with a variety of other responsibilities which they are ill equipped to fulfill. Manuscript editing, production supervision, and related tasks require skills that they have not acquired in the course of their academic training before assuming the responsibility for editing journals. Despite a good deal of self-help that goes on informally or among associations of editors, they think a systematic program of training, particularly for new editors, ought to be provided under the auspices of learned societies or universities—a suggestion that also merits consideration by foundations that are concerned about strengthening the scholarly communication system.

Perhaps the most unwelcome burden is the assortment of noneditorial tasks that on large journals are handled by marketing specialists and business managers. One promising solution—to be discussed in detail later in this chapter—is the forming of consortia so that these services can be consolidated. The Enquiry's survey found that three out of five editors (primarily those whose journals are not affiliated with learned societies) are willing to consider participation in a consortium, though few of them are ready to join without further clarification of important details of operation.

Overall, scholar–editors of medium-sized and small independent journals evince a mixture of pride in their mission and achievements and of disappointment in the failure of the scholarly community to recognize their problems and their contribution.

FINANCIAL PROBLEMS

The financial plight of many journals—especially small ones that are not affiliated with a scholarly society—has caused increasing concern. Rising costs confront every journal, and in a period of inflation a reasonable response is to raise prices. Declining circulation is a spotty problem. Not all journals are suffering from it. Nevertheless, for the long run, the major financial threat to journals, both those that are in strong condition today and those that are shaky, is the cancellation of library subscriptions because of budgetary constraints and a greater reliance on copying, interlibrary loans, or a national periodicals center, if it is established.

Journal publishers can improve their financial condition by increasing revenues, cutting costs, obtaining subsidies, or by a combination of these alternatives. What are the prospects in each area, particularly for the small independent journals?

IMPROVING REVENUES. Subscriptions are the major source of income for most journals, accounting for two-thirds or more of revenues, according to one survey (see table 2.2). For journals published by university presses, the figure was '79 percent, compared with 65 percent for commercial publishers. Dependence on subscriptions varies with the ability of the journal to attract advertising or to impose page charges.

Libraries on an average account for approximately half the subscriptions and close to two-thirds of the revenues of independent scholarly journals in the humanities and social sciences, according to the Enquiry's Survey of Editors. For large journals with several thousand subscribers and financed by membership dues, the proportion of library subscriptions is much lower and for expensive, commercial science journals it is higher. Among other journals, even within a discipline, there is a large variance in the ratio of individual to library subscriptions which probably reflects differences in the age of the journal, its prestige, price, and degree of specialization.

During a period of rising costs, changes in subscription rates offer the obvious way to increase revenues, but editors and publishers differ widely in their willingness to raise prices. Commercial publishers do not hesitate to do so, nor do major nonprofit publishers of a group of journals. But small independent journals have been apparently less willing to raise prices for fear of offending the editor's colleagues and of losing subscribers. Data on journal circulation and revenues, however, suggest that this fear is exaggerated. Circulation gains and losses seem to depend primarily on factors other than price. Journals can go broke not only by raising prices so rapidly that circulation falls off and total revenue declines, but also by holding prices almost constant while costs (and deficits) rise. There is no risk-free alternative; the advantage of the price-raising decision is that it at least offers a reasonable prospect of solvency.

If the Enquiry's Survey of Editors reflects nonprofit journals policy generally, it would appear that the financial difficulties encountered by small nonprofit journals during the 1970s are attributable in part to their failure to raise their prices fast enough. As table 2.3 indicates, the increases in rates

Table 2.2. Sources of Journal Revenue
(in percentages)

Source of funds	All publishers (137 journals)		Learned societies (72 journals)	University presses (25 journals)	Commercial publishers (40 journals)
	Number of journals receiving such revenue	Share of total revenue	Share of total revenue	Share of total revenue	Share of total revenue
Subscriptions	137	64.5	63.4	79.0	64.6
Page charges	30	8.3	13.2	0.0	0.0
Advertising	88	13.7	11.0	4.2	20.3
Sale of back issues	113	2.2	1.8	3.6	2.6
Sale of reprints	92	4.8	5.1	2.5	4.7
Sale of microform	57	1.1	1.6	0.2	0.0
Permission fees	22	0.0	0.0	0.9	0.0
All other	137	5.4	3.9	9.6	7.8
Total		100.0	100.0	100.0	100.0

Source: Based on data from Machlup, Leeson, and associates, table 3.4.13. The data are for 1974.

charged to individuals lagged substantially behind the rise in the general level of prices, and even the increases for institutional subscriptions kept pace with prices only in social sciences and literature, but not in philosophy.

Whether the Consumer Price Index is the best proxy for the increased costs actually encountered by the journals is uncertain, since printing, order fulfillment, and postage costs may rise at different rates from the average price of goods and services sampled by the government. But it is probably close enough to confirm the suspicion that journal editors and managers of small journals have been overly reluctant to raise their prices to individual subscribers. They were somewhat more willing to raise prices to libraries, but even so, prices for humanities journals have remained much lower than those in other fields, especially the sciences. King's report, for example, shows that average prices in 1975 of social sciences journals were $13.40 and $13.20, for institutions and individuals, respectively.[14] They were about five times as high—$77.50 and $58.10—for institutions and individuals subscribing to journals in the physical sciences. Average prices of scientific and technical journals were $31.50 for libraries and $27.50 for individuals, about double those for humanities journals. Crude comparisons among fields may be misleading, since scientific journals are costlier to produce. Still, publishers in the humanities are not in a great danger of pricing themselves out of the market if they raise their rates to keep pace with inflation. Yet it must be acknowledged that scholars answering the Enquiry's questionnaire did identify high prices as a major complaint. What is not clear is whether scholars were indicating more than a general complaint against inflation.

Fortunately, despite the increases in price, circulation was rising during the 1970s. From 1972 to 1977 the number of subscribers to literature journals covered in the Enquiry's Survey of Editors rose 44 percent for individuals and 13 percent for institutions. In the social sciences the gains were only 7 percent for individuals and 12 percent for institutions. In philosophy individual subscriptions dropped 9 percent, but institutional subscriptions rose 8 percent. Over the 1966–75 period, a survey of forty-three journals by Machlup and others shows a 17 percent increase in circulation; for the four humanities journals in that survey, the increase was 42 percent. Thus both surveys suggest that price is less decisive than is widely assumed. Modest increases seem to be tolerated.

14. King Research, Inc., *A Chartbook of Indicators of Scientific and Technical Communication in the United States*. (Washington, D.C., National Science Foundation, 1977) p. 13.

Table 2.3. Changes in the Consumer Price Index (CPI) and Selected Average Journal Prices, 1970–77

| | Year | | Percentage |
	1970	1977	change
Consumer Price Index (1967＝100)	116.3	181.5	65
Subscription price for individuals			
Philosophy	$ 7.91	$10.47	32
Literature	6.00	9.00	50
Social sciences	7.33	11.13	52
Subscription price for institutions			
Philosophy	$10.00	$15.23	52
Literature	6.57	10.90	66
Social sciences	8.00	17.29	116

Sources: National Enquiry Survey of Editors, unpublished, and Bureau of Labor Statistics.

To some extent, the timid price policy of the editors surveyed may reflect their greater interest in maintaining individual subscriptions, whereas commercial journals, seeking to maximize revenue rather than subscribers, have typically based their charges on the library market that has generally been less sensitive to price. But since periodic price increases are unavoidable in an inflationary economy, editors and business managers should set their prices at a level that will reduce their deficits, if possible, and certainly high enough to prevent a worsening of their situation. One wonders whether a more aggressive pricing strategy—if properly explained and accompanied by a more active promotion policy—might work out to a journal's advantage.

A successful promotional campaign aimed at justifying higher subscription rates and at attracting new subscribers should be linked, we think, not only to the usefulness of a journal to scholars as readers, but to scholars as authors. So long as scholars are dependent on publication for their advancement, they have a great stake in the survival of journals in which they might publish. Furthermore, scholars share in the general responsibility which falls in part on universities, foundations, government, and so on to support scholarly enterprises for altruistic reasons related to their professional commitment. The Enquiry's interviews with scholars indicate that this responsibility is widely recognized. Many scholars indicated that they already maintain subscriptions, not because they are interested in a journal's content, but because they believe the journal should be supported as a contribution to scholarship.

For years, journal editors lived with the comforting illusion that there would always be enough library subscriptions to sustain their operations, but now they recognize that they can no longer do so. The changing financial circumstances of libraries have put an end to complacence. Increasing competition for the library dollar has already affected the circulation of some journals. To offset this loss, new efforts should be made to sell more subscriptions to individual scholars by methods such as those discussed in this chapter. A regular program of promotion is an essential part of journal publishing. There is much skepticism about the success of promotional efforts among many editors of independent journals, whereas among some publishers of groups of journals, who have succeeded in attracting new individual subscribers, there is a strong commitment to vigorous promotion.

For a single journal the costs of such an effort—rental of mailing lists, preparation of circulars, mailing and postage, and so on, would be excessive. But for a group of journals, perhaps with the cooperation of a learned society, it would be manageable. This is one of several areas in which joint efforts can pay off.

A number of other conventional marketing tactics also merit trial. For example:

- A special rate for group orders—say, three or more copies sent to a single address, such as the department office
- Lower rates for multiple-year subscriptions
- Special introductory rates for subscribers to other journals
- Joint offers that give a lower rate for ordering two or more journals
- Encouragement of purchases by departments of highly specialized journals, with costs shared by interested faculty members.

Presumably some editors can increase subscriptions by improving the quality of their journals. Some editorial initiatives—timelier publication, for example, or more effective use of summaries—may also help build circulation.

Recommendation 2.4. Promotion of subscriptions
We recommend that journals intensify their efforts to build circulation among individual scholars.

Advertising, which is an important source of revenue for larger, more established journals, especially in the sciences, makes little contribution to the revenue of most humanities journals. Nor is there much prospect that humanities journals will be able to improve their advertising income.

Submission fees, on the other hand, do deserve serious consideration. They are warranted in principle because each article submitted imposes a cost—on the journal editor, on referees, and on the clerical staff. They can also be defended on the grounds that since publication may be undertaken at least in part to advance the status of the author, it seems logical to call on the author to help pay the cost. (Some observers have suggested that submission fees should be refunded if the article is accepted, but this would not be sensible if the primary purpose is to raise revenues. The cost of handling the manuscript occurs irrespective of acceptance. For the successful author, acceptance is a sufficient return on the investment.)

If submission fees are logical and desirable, why have they not been tried more widely? One reason is that journal editors have disliked the notion in principle. They oppose financial obstacles to publication—especially for younger scholars. Moreover, there is a widespread belief that unless submission fees are imposed universally in a discipline, they will not be feasible. A journal that imposes submission fees, it is argued, will be avoided by authors so long as free access is available to other journals in the field. What this suggests is that submission fees will be successful only if most journals—or at least the leading journals—in a field impose them.

If successful, a submission fee would not by itself be the answer to the financial problems of journals. Its potential is limited. But for a small journal, the annual income from one hundred submission fees of, say, $25 each, might make the difference between staying in business and bankruptcy.

While publishers, editors, and scholars in the humanities have debated the feasibility of submission fees, the practice has quietly spread in other fields, such as economics and sociology. Several years ago the *American Economic Review*, the research journal of the American Economic Association, introduced a $15 submission fee for members and $30 for nonmembers. It was proposed by the editor not so much for raising revenues as for improving the refereeing process. The fees provide a modest sum to pay selected recent Ph.D.s for preliminary screening of manuscripts. Not only were these young scholars directly helpful to the editor, but by virtue of the experience they obtained, they prepared themselves for later service as referees or perhaps as editors.

The impact of the change on submissions was slight. The number of manuscripts submitted declined somewhat, but not the quality—which may indicate that some authors who routinely submitted manuscripts to the *American Economic Review* first began to assess more realistically their chances of acceptance.

Several other economics journals now also employ submission fees. For example, *The Journal of Political Economy*, one of the most prestigious journals in the field, charges a $30 submission fee and explicitly earmarks the proceeds for refereeing. *The Journal of Finance* charges $20; *Economic Enquiry* (the journal of the Western Economic Association) charges members $25 and nonmembers $60. In England, the *Economic Journal* charges $22.50 for manuscripts by nonmembers. A number of journals, however, continue to publish without submission fees—thus casting doubt on the notion that submission fees must be universal to be workable. Other social sciences are also following this practice. For example, *The American Sociologist*, journal of the American Sociological Association, charges a processing fee of $10 but waives it for students. Five other journals published by the association also follow the same policy.

The submission fee has been justified sometimes on the grounds of improving and paying for services that were formerly rendered without charge, or on the grounds that there is no reason for an association to extend the same service to nonmembers as to members. The linking of a submission fee to an improved service bears out a finding of the Enquiry's Survey of Scholars: a majority of those interviewed said they would be willing to pay a $35 submission fee if by so doing they could make multiple submissions. Whether the scholars would accept as willingly a submission fee intended solely to raise revenue has not been established by the foregoing evidence, but if the alternative to a submission fee of, say, $25, is the demise of the journal, it is reasonable to hypothesize that keeping the journal alive may also be considered a useful service.

Recommendation 2.5. Submission fees
We recommend that journals impose submission fees either to raise revenues or to provide modest compensation for referees.

Although scholars appear to be willing to pay for the privilege of submitting their articles to several journals simultaneously, such payments would not necessarily assure more rapid publication. Indeed, the consequences of multiple submissions might be quite the opposite. It might reduce efficiency by imposing a much greater burden on the refereeing process. If all articles are submitted simultaneously to only two publications, for example, each one will be read twice, whereas at the present time, they are read an average of 1.5 times, as indicated earlier.

What is needed is not multiple submissions, which increase the burden, but selective submissions. Rejection rates might be lowered if authors had a better understanding of the policies of journals in their discipline. The need for better information about the journal market (as well as of the policies of book publishers) was strongly reflected in responses to the Enquiry's Survey of Scholars. Some associations, notably the Modern Language Association (MLA), have sought to respond to this need, and further efforts by others would clearly be welcomed.

Page charges have been widely accepted by science and technology journals when they can be recovered from a research grant. When paid, they average more than $300 an article. But they seem less acceptable when they must be paid by the individual scholar. We consider them to be less desirable than submission fees.[15]

Subsidies play a significant role in financing many journals. Generally, they are indirect—free rent from a university and time contributed by the editor and other staff members. These are substantial and, if they were priced out, might exceed the income from subscriptions. They will continue to play an essential role in the survival of scholarly journals. Whether additional subsidies are warranted seems dubious. By and large, journals that are already receiving a substantial indirect subsidy and are still unable to pay their way, probably ought not to be published—or at least not published in a way that makes it impossible for them to break even. If revenues are not adequate, costs should be cut and alternative publishing arrangements explored before additional subsidies are considered.

15. Page charges were initiated by *The Physical Review* about 1932 at $2 per published page and have risen to more than $70 a page. The rationale for the page charge, which was set to cover editorial and composition costs, was the belief that research is not complete until it is published. Subscription costs were kept low because they had to cover only the costs of production, primarily paper and press work, and distribution costs. Page charges were always assessed against the author's institution, not the author. The system worked well as long as research was well funded. When budgets tightened, payments for page charges declined precipitously. Many journals in the sciences then introduced a two-track system—relatively rapid publication (within six months) for those who paid, and delayed publication (up to two years) for those who did not. (Adapted from a note from Arthur Herschman of the American Association for the Advancement of Science, former editor of *The Physical Review*.)

The impact of the new copyright law on journal revenues and growth is difficult to predict without more information on the use of photocopying and on how scholars, libraries, and publishers adapt to the new guidelines of the law. But it would be unduly optimistic to expect photocopying fees to have a marked impact on journal finances.

In 1978 the nonprofit Copyright Clearance Center, Inc. (CCC) was established to promote easier access to copyrighted works and payment of publishers and authors for the use of the materials in accord with the new revisions of the copyright law.[16] The center provides a mechanism for the collection of fees for publishers and the processing of reports and remittances made by users when copying exceeds CONTU guidelines.

The CCC has drafted a sample notice to appear in each journal registered with the center to explain the fee-payment method. Since scholars should be familiar with the notice, it is reproduced below.

The appearance of the code at the bottom of the first page of an article in this journal indicates the copyright owner's consent that copies of the article may be made for personal or internal use, or for personal or internal use of specific clients. This consent is given on the condition, however, that the copier pay the stated per-copy fee through the Copyright Clearance Center, Inc., P.O. Box 765, Schenectady, New York 12301, for copying beyond that permitted by Sections 107 or 108 of the U.S. Copyright Law. This consent does not extend to other kinds of copying, such as copying for general distribution, for advertising or promotional purposes, for creating new collective works, or for resale.

More than 2,200 journals and serials, 800 libraries and other users, and 200 publishers had registered in the program by early 1979. The average payment for an article has been $1.50, of which 25 cents is kept by the Center. A few individuals who do extensive copying are also registered, but by and large individuals are expected to send checks directly to the Center in accord with instructions appearing in the copying notice. Up to 1979 nearly all of the cooperating publications were scientific and technical journals.

16. The new U.S. Copyright Law, public law 94-553, was enacted in 1976 and went into effect January 1, 1978. The law provides for single-copy reproduction by libraries and teachers under certain conditions but requires payment for systematic copying or copying for commercial advantage. See R. 21, *Reproduction of Copyrighted Works by Educators and Librarians*, (Washington, D.C., Library of Congress, Copyright Office, 1978) and *Photocopying by Academic, Public and Nonprofit Research Libraries* (Washington, D.C., Association of American Publishers, May 1978). For additional information, publishers and users should write to the Copyright Clearance Center, P.O. Box 8891, Boston, MA 02114.

Only a handful of journals in the humanities registered, among them *Scholarly Publishing*.

Not surprisingly, therefore, corporate libraries and other business users are the best customers of the center so far. Among university librarians there is a widespread belief that most copying by university libraries falls within the CONTU guidelines and that payments from nonprofit libraries are likely to be relatively small. Meanwhile, much casual copying by individuals continues without payment of royalties, as does quantity copying of material for classroom use, purchased from commercial copying services. Individuals who would be willing to cooperate with the copyright clearance system either are not fully aware of what to do or find compliance a nuisance; those who understand the law but ignore it can easily escape detection. Clearly there is a need to educate the scholarly community regarding the role of the center and to enforce copyright policy more effectively. Government or foundation support of the center's efforts to become a self-supporting institution, if needed during its initial stages, would be warranted.

Some speculations on the impact of the new copyright guidelines on journal finances suggest that

– If library subscriptions are cut back as a result of an increase in photocopying, the impact may be disproportionately heavy on the humanities because scientists are perceived to be less tolerant of delays in the acquisition of needed articles.

– The transaction costs of fulfilling a request for a single on-demand article (about $3 to $4 each) are much higher than the royalty payment. A dollar spent by a library for acquiring articles on demand will contribute less in royalty revenue to the publisher than a dollar spent on journal subscriptions. The National Technical Information Service, the federal agency which experimented for a year in providing a "journal article copy service," charged a $6.50 fee, of which 50 cents was identified as a royalty payment. Thus, as acquisition by libraries of single copies increases, as it has in the recent past, then net revenues to scholarly journals as a group will decrease. Foreign specialty journals, however, are more likely to be affected than domestic ones.

– The higher the royalty payment in relation to the subscription price for a journal, the smaller the loss of subscriptions—a proposition that has led some commercially published journals in science to set very high royalty payments per article.

– Humanistic journals are less likely to derive significant revenues from royalties than science journals, which are given multiple use in a large number of industrial libraries. But if the photocopying revenues contribute to stability in the price of science journals, then humanistic journals may perhaps retain a more equitable share in academic library allocations.

Some editors and publishers are cooperating with the center primarily because they support the principle of compensating authors and journals for the use of their materials. They are not optimistic yet about the amount of income that can be earned. One estimate is that 1 or 2 percent of a journal's revenues may be obtained from photocopying.[17]

Recommendation 2.6.   Cooperation with the Copyright Clearance Center
We recommend that scholarly journals, libraries, and scholars cooperate with the Copyright Clearance Center in order to simplify the dissemination of scholarly information and compensate copyright owners for the use of copyrighted material.

DIFFERENTIAL PRICING.   There has been much discussion about the economics and fairness of differential subscription rates for institutions (chiefly libraries) and individuals. We cannot judge the appropriateness of the practice in all circumstances, but we believe that, in principle, a modest differential is justified for several reasons, and that a digression to explore the advantages and disadvantages of the system is warranted. The case for a dual price system is as follows:

1. Individual subscribers are single readers, whereas library copies are read by many. It is not illogical to recognize the number of probable readings as a factor in price, especially since the availability of copies in a library may reduce the number of individual subscriptions.[18]

2. Library subscriptions are frequently placed through subscription agencies which customarily charge publishers a commission of 15 to 20 percent for handling library orders. From the viewpoint of the publisher, the

17. A. F. Spilhaus, Jr., "The Copyright Clearance Center," *Scholarly Publishing* (January 1978).

18. An example taken from the experience of Heldref—a nonprofit publisher discussed at length later in this report—is illuminating. When Heldref launched two book review journals, it obtained in response to its initial mailing to academics about 1,700 subscribers to each journal. Only about 100 in each group were institutional subscribers. Over a period of five years, the

service provided by subscription agencies benefits libraries more than publishers, since it enables libraries to consolidate their journal orders into a
single transaction. Thus, the differential price can be viewed in part as a
device for putting the service charge back on the libraries. (The subscription
agency is the incidental beneficiary of such an increase, since the higher
price means a higher commission, assuming the commission rate remains
the same.)

For these two reasons alone a differential of perhaps 50 percent between
institutional and individual subscriptions does not seem out of line. Many
humanities journals do not charge a differential or, if they do, it is a smaller
one.

There is, in addition, an economic rationale for a dual price system, and
it is employed widely in the private market for goods and services. It is based
on the fact that for many products separate groups of buyers can be identified
who are willing to buy the product at different prices. Thus, adults and
children can be charged different prices for admission to movies, for trans-
portation, and so on. The result of charging such fees is to increase total
revenues by increasing the patronage of children without reducing income
from the patronage of adults. Indeed, the lower rate for children is likely to
encourage greater travel and movie-going by adults. The differential is easy
to administer—few adults can pass as children—and because it is in line with
people's notion of fairness, it persists without challenge.

The economic rationale for dual subscription rates is similar. The basic
subscription rate is the rate for libraries, and it is set by taking into account
the costs of production and the probable number of buyers.

Thus, a publisher might think that it is possible to break even on the
production of 2,000 copies of a journal at a subscription price of $20 a year.
At this rate (assuming that the journal is not distributed as part of membership in an organization) library orders may account for three out of four
subscriptions.

------

number of library subscriptions rose steadily, and the number of individual subscriptions
steadily dropped. Today four out of five subscriptions are institutional subscriptions, and the
total number of subscriptions has dropped slightly. Dollar income has been maintained since
institutions pay a higher rate than individuals. Heldref's explanation of this pattern is that
individual scholars tried out the new journal and then asked their departments or libraries to pick
up the subscription thereafter. Heldref's view is that a 50 percent differential is justified to
compensate for multiple reading in libraries and the 15 to 20 percent commission charged by
subscription agencies.

But suppose the publisher believes, on the basis of market studies or hunch, that, at a price of $10 a year, sales to individuals might reach 1,500 copies instead of 500. The net revenue would be changed as follows. Income would be reduced by $5,000 because the 500 individual subscribers willing to pay $20 would be paying only $10 instead. But this loss of $5,000 would be more than offset by the gain of $10,000 from the sale of 1,000 additional subscriptions. If the cost of printing and distributing the additional 1,000 subscriptions is less than $5,000, it would pay the publisher to institute a dual pricing system, since his net revenues would increase.

The other groups would also benefit. The original group of individual buyers would obtain their subscription at a 50 percent saving, and 1,000 additional buyers would be able to get the journal at the price they are willing to pay. In some circumstances the additional income from sales to individuals might permit a reduction in the price charged to libraries. Most important for the purpose of scholarly communication, the distribution of knowledge will have been enhanced.

Heavy criticism of the dual subscription approach has come from those who think that frequently the rate charged individual subscribers is the rate that is necessary to make the journal self-supporting, and that an additional charge is imposed on libraries, which yields a windfall profit. The pricing of some technical and scientific journals at rates several times as high as those charged individuals has also been attacked. The legality of the two-tier system has also been called into question by the Internal Revenue Service, which views the lower price for members of a professional society as a subsidy for members and inconsistent with the preferential tax status for professional societies.

The extent to which libraries have been exploited or individuals subsidized is not clear. The unusually rapid rise in some journal prices has been a problem for libraries, however. We think the problem results from efforts by some publishers to charge all that the traffic will bear and from uncritical purchasing by librarians rather than from the dual price system itself. The dual system can abet exploitive practices, however, since a cheap rate for individuals keeps scholars happy—particularly the scholars participating in the production of the journals.

It is an interesting anomaly that journal and book publishers have adopted diametrically opposite policies in their approach to library sales. While journal publishers charge higher prices to libraries than to individuals, many book publishers offer discounts, often 10 or 20 percent of list price to libraries, particularly if libraries are willing to place a standing order for part of or all of a scholarly publisher's output, or purchase a number of titles at one time. It is perhaps even more interesting to note that both policies seem to work. Even more remarkable—and a notable testament to the law-abiding world of scholarship—is the fact that scholars do not buy their books through libraries, and libraries do not buy their journals through scholars in order to get the lower price.

COST-CUTTING AND COOPERATIVE ARRANGEMENTS.   Costs can be cut either by efficiencies that do not visibly alter the product, by a deliberate reduction in quality, or by economies of scale through cooperative efforts.

It is very difficult to determine what a journal with certain characteristics should cost. Editors have no easy, sure-fire way to determine whether they are paying too much for particular services. A number of studies of journal costs have been made, but figures seem to defy generalization and comparison. For example, comparisons of composition costs per page are often meaningless since they generally are not standardized for type size, line width, and depth of the text page. Comparisons of costs by function—manufacturing, editorial, fulfillment, and so on—are distorted by indirect subsidies such as contributions of editorial time or office space and utilities. Costs for a single publication may be difficult to identify in organizations that publish several journals.

We know of no guidelines that can serve as a handy reference for editors. But editors can surely benefit from comparing cost experiences. In some disciplines, informal exchanges of cost and other information are made at workshops and symposia conducted in conjunction with annual meetings of learned societies.

Ultimately, there is no substitute for obtaining competitive quotations from different printers for various types of composition, paper, and printing.

Another route to cost reduction is the deliberate sacrifice of quality as it is conventionally measured. For example, authors whose papers have been accepted can be required to submit camera-ready copy—manuscripts typed in accord with specifications established by the journal. This practice is now extensive among a number of highly specialized journals and book publishers. It greatly reduces editorial and proofing costs and eliminates composition costs, typically the single largest cost for small journals.

This method of cost-cutting need not affect the refereeing process or the quality of technical editing, but it does reduce the esthetic attractiveness of a journal—a matter that appears to be of greater concern to journal authors and editors than to journal readers. Authors' objections may possibly be overcome by maintaining the credibility of the journal's peer review process and by encouraging university administrators to put greater emphasis on article quality than on the prestige or appearance of a journal in the evaluation of faculty for advancement. Commercial publishers, especially in the sciences, appear to be more willing to accept this comp.omise than are scholars, especially those in the humanities. Cost reduction through cooperative action or through more effective management may offer the best opportunity for reducing operating deficits of small journals.

The advantages of publishing several journals jointly instead of separately are evident from the financial health and growth of large multijournal producers such as the major scientific and engineering societies, the American Psychological Association, Sage Publications, the University of Chicago Press, and other university publishers. While most journals in the humanities and humanistic social sciences are produced singly—about 90 percent of them, as shown in table 2.4—there has been a notable increase during the past decade in multijournal producers such as Scholars Press, Heldref Publications, and the American Anthropological Association. The formation of additional consortia in philosophy, literature, and sociology is under consideration. Furthermore, the existing consortia continue to add new journals. The opportunity for further consolidation is suggested by the tabulation in table 2.4.

The two different approaches, which are illustrated by Heldref and the American Anthropological Association, warrant further discussion because they illustrate that the economies from consolidation of publishing operations can make it possible for small journals of even a few hundred subscribers to survive.

Heldref was founded in 1971 in Washington, D.C., by the Helen Dwight Reid Educational Foundation because the foundation's president believed that many small but useful and well established journals were threatened with extinction unless they could be operated more efficiently.[19] In the ensuing seven years Heldref became the publisher for twenty-three journals that were in financial difficulty. In 1978, when it grossed nearly $1 million, Heldref more than covered direct costs and overhead costs. All but one publication covered direct costs (editorial, composition, printing, mail-

19. Interview with Cornelius W. Vahle, Jr., director, Heldref Publications.

Table 2.4. Distribution of Journals Among Publishers in the United States, 1973

1,409 publishers published	1 journal each, or altogether	1,409 journals
115 publishers published	2 journals each, or altogether	230 journals
38 publishers published	3 journals each, or altogether	114 journals
20 publishers published	4 journals each, or altogether	80 journals
12 publishers published	5 journals each, or altogether	60 journals
7 publishers published	6 journals each, or altogether	42 journals
6 publishers published	7 journals each, or altogether	42 journals
2 publishers published	8 journals each, or altogether	16 journals
3 publishers published	9 journals each, or altogether	27 journals
1 publisher published	10 journals	10 journals
3 publishers published	11 journals each, or altogether	33 journals
3 publishers published	12 journals each, or altogether	36 journals
1 publisher published	13 journals	13 journals
2 publishers published	14 journals each, or altogether	28 journals
2 publishers published	15 journals each, or altogether	30 journals
1 publisher published	18 journals	18 journals
1 publisher published	22 journals	22 journals
3 publishers published	24 journals each, or altogether	72 journals
1 publisher published	25 journals	25 journals
2 publishers published	26 journals each, or altogether	52 journals
1 publisher published	36 journals	36 journals
1 publisher published	64 journals	64 journals
1,634 publishers published	altogether	2,459 journals

Source: Fritz Machlup, Kenneth W. Leeson, and associates, *Information Through the Printed Word: The Dissemination of Scholarly, Scientific, and Intellectual Knowledge* (New York, New York University, March 15, 1978) processed.

ing and postage). Most of them broke even entirely and several of them contributed more than their share. As a nonprofit publisher, Heldref is willing to carry a publication that is not covering its share of the overhead, if it believes in the usefulness of the publication and if the venture as a whole is breaking even.

Heldref's policy is to buy journals at a modest fee and assume responsibility for their production and distribution. However, it often leaves control of editorial policy to the originating organization. *Germanic Review*, for example, which now breaks even on a circulation of 1,200, was purchased from the Columbia University Press when Columbia decided to discontinue its journals operation, and *Historical Methods* (800 subscribers) was obtained from the University of Pittsburgh. *Germanic Review* is a refereed journal that is under the editorial control of a distinguished editorial board, but all publishing decisions—format, production, price, and so forth—are made by Heldref.

Not all of Heldref's publications would be viewed as scholarly under a strict definition of the term. But all are educational, and all require academic editorial direction. One of the latest acquisitions—*Environment*, which originated at Washington University and which is published in cooperation with the Scientists' Institute for Public Information—is a magazine written by scholars for a wider public. *Poet Lore*, established in 1889, publishes original poetry for a small readership of 400.

In deciding whether to select a journal, Heldref takes into account several factors. It prefers established journals that have demonstrated usefulness and quality, the contents must be scholarly or educational and under the direction of qualified scholars, and they must show potential for meeting direct costs. The final requirement—that Heldref serve as publisher—has led some journals that wanted publishing services to forgo joining the program because they wanted to retain control over production and pricing.

The fact that a number of journals wanted the benefit of Heldref's services but did not want to relinquish the publisher's prerogative suggests that there is need for another type of nonprofit organization—one that provides services but that leaves publishing decisions to the sponsoring group.

The American Anthropological Association (AAA) provides such services for eight other anthropological learned societies which collectively produce about seventy issues a year.[20] The cooperative venture began with the AAA assuming dues billing and record maintenance responsibilities for the other societies. Accounting services were added, and then composition and production services followed after the AAA set up its own composition operation in 1970 in an effort to cope with rapidly rising costs.

Another alternative is the establishment of a new consortium. Whatever the arrangement, however, the editorial function and refereeing continue to be decentralized, with the scholar–editors in charge.

Services may be comprehensive—including editing, composition, printing, and fulfillment as provided by AAA—or they may be selective, covering only one or two steps in the publishing process. For example, a

20. Personal communication from Edward J. Lehman, executive director of the American Anthropological Association.

Cooperative Editorial Facility that will use computers and photocomposition technology for editing and the preparation of camera-ready copy is being developed by Joseph Raben.[21] With a grant from the Carnegie Corporation, Raben has embarked on a three-year program that will be in full operation in 1982. Fifteen journals have indicated an interest in this service.

Can we identify the reasons why twenty-three formerly independent journals, all of which were in financial difficulty, could become successful when consolidated by Heldref? Some part of the organization's success must be attributed to excellence of leadership and management. Savings in composition costs, the largest single item of expense, have been significant. Composition, which is simple, but professional and highly readable, is done in-house—most of it with sophisticated strike-on equipment used by highly skilled operators, at an estimated savings of 50 percent over the cost of purchase of similar composition on the outside. Subscription lists, maintained by a service organization, are kept up to date from a terminal at the Heldref office. In short, Heldref succeeds not because it has discovered a panacea for journal publishing, but because it employs the best established practices. The same generalization applies to the AAA.

What might happen if a cluster of small journals pooled their fulfillment and management efforts or obtained them from a single well-established journal publisher?

– Production costs might be reduced if the type, makeup, and paper specifications for a number of small journals were coordinated to facilitate composition and production, and if a single printer handled a cluster of publications.

– A single computerized fulfillment program might reduce the number of separate accounts and attendant processing costs, generate renewal notices to maintain subscription records, facilitate market research to increase subscriptions, and make reader surveys to define the need for new services. Moreover, a consortium allows an on-going observation of opportunities for starting new journals or merging journals when there is significant overlap in both content and subscribers.

– A consortium could afford full-time specialists in pricing, promotion, and fulfillment and encourage greater flexibility and expertise in

21. Raben, a professor of English at Queens College of the City University of New York, founded the quarterly international journal, *Computers and the Humanities*, in 1966 and has been supported in earlier studies of computer applications by grants from the Alfred P. Sloan Foundation and the Andrew W. Mellon Foundation.

planning, using new technology and experimenting with innovative modifications.

A consortium could make a major service to member journals by providing a manual of style for all journals in the group, initiating manuscript submission fees, standardizing reference citations and key-word descriptions to aid future retrieval, eliminating expensive composition formats, and encouraging submission of machine-readable manuscripts. These changes, which anticipate future automation, can be greatly facilitated by a large multijournal producer within a discipline.

Although the style manual is a logical by-product of a consortium, it could be undertaken as well by a learned society or by an association of editors. *The MLA Handbook* serves this function for the language field, for example, and the American Philosophical Association has also provided a guidebook for its field.[22]

Despite the increase in the number of scholarly journals obtaining publishing services from consortia of one kind or another, many journal editors have reservations about participating. In the Enquiry survey, editors were asked whether they would be willing to participate in forming a consortium with similar journals. Of those responding, 40 percent said no, 48 percent said maybe, and 12 percent replied yes. The responses, while mixed, indicate sufficient interest to initiate a consortium in each of the disciplines surveyed.

The principal stated objections to joining a consortium are fears of red tape and loss of control. Personal interviews also revealed another problem. Many independent scholarly journals operate with substantial hidden subsidies from a department or university. Participation in a consortium would mean that these would be replaced by explicit payments for services. Such explicit support would be an exposed amount vulnerable to elimination during some future budget crisis. Thus, some assurances of funds to cover subsidy losses may be a necessary condition for gaining support for a

---

22. In 1975 the American Philosophical Association published *Guidebook for Publishing Philosophy*, a seventy-five-page publication prepared by Janice Moulton of the Department of Psychology, Duke University. It combines a style guide with information about policies of individual journals. For a comprehensive guide to editorial policies and manuscript submission requirements, see the *Directory of Publishing Opportunities in Journals and Periodicals* (4th ed., Chicago, Marquis Academic Media, 1979). The directory lists 3,483 journals and periodicals, including foreign publications accepting manuscripts in English.

consortium. There will be little incentive for an editor to reduce costs if the savings are more than offset by the loss of subsidies.

Many of the expected benefits of a consortium will be increased if the journals share some overlapping groups of authors and subscribers. The learned society or association is the most logical center for integrating the published literature in a discipline. It is in a strong position to assume leadership in cooperative efforts and to seek foundation help for pilot efforts.

Recommendation 2.7.   Economies for small journals
We recommend that small independent journals seek production, subscription fulfillment, and other services from large established journals, university presses, or other oganizations that can offer the economies that small operations cannot obtain on their own.

JOURNAL SUBSTITUTES AND SUPPLEMENTS
Leadership in the search for alternatives to the traditional journal and modifications of it have come from the sciences and technology where higher costs (complex typesetting in mathematics or chemistry, for example), the need for speedy dissemination, and the presence of an industrial or defense-related market segment have provided ample funds for experiment and innovation. The development of computerized bibliographical references and indexes, the use of word processing equipment and optical scanners, and the extension of microfiche service have moved ahead substantially. Several variations in format and packaging have also been tried out. Nonetheless, the number of conventional scientific and technical journals has continued to increase at the same time. Thus, what appears to be taking place is not displacement of journals by alternatives, but rather the introduction of modifications or supplementary services.[23]

One criticism leveled against the journal system is that it performs its dissemination function inefficiently. A journal's scope may be so broad that

23. *Improving the Dissemination of Scientific and Technical Information: A Practitioner's Guide to Innovation*, prepared by Capital Systems Group, Inc. for the Office of Science Information Service, National Science Foundation. A looseleaf publication with entries from the period 1975–78, this excellent publication is not only a useful guide to new technology, but a useful reference on other aspects of editing and publishing. Editors and others concerned about scholarly communication may be interested in a new organization, the Society for Scholarly Publishing. Established in early 1979, it seeks to promote communication across disciplinary lines and among different publishing enterprises. Address: Suite LL, 1909 K Street, N.W., Washington, D.C., 20006.

only a few of the published articles are relevant to any one reader's interest. Or a journal may not be comprehensive enough; consequently, the subscriber has to search many journals or bibliographies to obtain all or most of the articles he needs to read. A number of proposals have been made in response to these criticisms.

SELECTIVE DISSEMINATION. Since only a few articles in each issue interest the average subscriber, there is considerable wastage in printing, paper, and postage. To conserve on these items, the feasibility of tailor-made journals for each reader has been tested in the sciences. Subscribers, grouped by computer-produced profiles of their interests, were sent selected lists of articles from a group of journals and were given a choice of what they wanted to receive. Unfortunately, this experiment in improving the "precision" of dissemination proved uneconomical. The additional cost was greater than the savings from the elimination of waste. Moreover, there was a loss in convenience. The *Annals of IEEE* service failed eventually because few engineers were willing to purchase individual articles on a regular basis— that is, unrelated to specific research needs and in lieu of a journal subscription. This experiment may not be the conclusive answer for all fields for all time, but it strongly suggests that the added costs of cataloging articles and preparing interest profiles are high enough to discourage humanists from buying such a service. The loss of convenience might be an even bigger obstacle.

Another way to improve article selection is to send subscribers abstracts or a table of contents and invite them to order individually (or on demand) the articles they choose. The Society for Automotive Engineers has been doing this successfully for a number of years, having done away with the conventional journal.

While such a system may work for the technologist whose needs for information are very specific and focused on specific problems rather than on broad subjects, it is unlikely to be attractive to a humanist with broad interests who probably would rather pay $3 to acquire thirty articles in a journal (several of which he may read or scan, now or in the future) than to pay $3 for a single article. In short, the single journal article may be too small a unit to be sold economically because of the large transaction costs involved. Such on-demand requests are more suited for special needs than for regular scholarly reading.

A more promising type of selective dissemination—introduced primarily to cope with the oversupply of accepted manuscripts—is the synoptic publishing approach adopted by the *Journal of Modern History*. In every issue it includes synopses of three or four very specialized articles reproduced from the author's typescript. The full text of the articles can be ordered either separately or (at a discount) as a yearly subscription. While demand for individual articles is low—not surprising since the price is $5 an article—300 libraries subscribe to the yearly collection so that scholars at these institutions have the option of using the library copy instead of purchasing individual articles.

The *Journal of Modern History* uses this publishing format to preserve its broad focus as well as to reduce its backlog by overcoming space limitations. While the journal has been successful in its efforts, questions have been raised whether less-prestigious journals will be able to coax authors to provide camera-ready copy and to consent to publication in a synoptic format, suffering a greatly diminished audience as a consequence. But status may be more important than readership. The Survey of Scholars found that two out of three authors are willing to accept synoptic publishing if it is refereed and recognized by faculty evaluation committees as the equivalent of conventional publishing.

The Enquiry's Survey of Scholars indicates that authors are willing to accept synoptic publishing so long as their articles are appropriately reviewed and accepted by their departments as fully accredited publications. The extension of a journal's reach by synoptic publishing may reduce the pressure for creation of additional journals that may not be financially viable. Moreover, it offers flexibility. The number of articles summarized can be increased or decreased more readily than can the number of articles in the journal.

Recommendation 2.8.   Alternatives to conventional publications
    We recommend that journals explore the possibilities of synoptic publishing and other alternatives to conventional procedures so that they can continue to make highly specialized scholarship more readily available at little additional cost.

A variation of the synoptic scheme would be the immediate publication in a journal of abstracts of all articles that have been accepted in a given time period, with the offer to make them available on-demand in typescript. Articles that are most likely to be read by the subscribers, or for which the requests are the highest, would be published in full text in the next issue along with the new abstracts. At the end of the year, the on-demand articles that remain unpublished could be packaged and sold as a bundle. Such a procedure rapidly announces articles and certifies them for tenure decisions, dissociates the certification function of the journal from dissemination, and provides some feedback on subscriber preferences to the editor.

The dual journal approach is another proposal for improving efficiency. The full text of articles is made available only through a library edition of the journal. The edition for individuals carries synoptics. Such an experiment was tried by the American Chemical Society, with mixed results. The society realized a 30 percent reduction in composition costs by printing the full-text articles in the library edition from author-prepared camera-ready copy, and this was the major attractiveness of the dual journal format. It is a roundabout way of getting subscribers to accept uncomposed or author-composed publication and offers no special advantage to humanists.

By publishing synoptics instead of full text, the small-circulation journal in the humanities is likely to save only a modest amount in paper and printing. The principal savings could be achieved independently of the decision to publish synoptics. For a large-circulation journal, composition costs per subscriber are small and the principal costs are printing and paper. Thus, in its decision to publish an article, the journal must evaluate the number of subscribers interested in the full text of the article and compare the cost of 10 cents for a ten-page article sold as an inclusion in the journal (going to all subscribers) versus $5 for supplying a single article on-demand.

Another variation of the dual journal approach is the publication of conventional journals for libraries and reprint journals for individuals. The reprint journals would be initiated solely to improve dissemination. By reprinting by photo offset articles from overlapping journals, such a publication could provide a group of scholars with a custom-made journal that offers comprehensive coverage of a well defined topic. For example, in 1975, twenty articles on George Eliot appeared in as many different journals. To sell them individually at the on-demand price of $3 or more each would be prohibitive, but they could be sold profitably as a package or as an annual collection, if enough scholars are particularly interested in George Eliot and can be identified as a market.

INTERIM DISSEMINATION. A well-established way to deal with the problem of delay is the publication of working paper series. These series are common in university departments in sciences and social sciences, in private research institutions, and government agencies, but not in humanities departments.

Working papers are typically copies of a typed manuscript with a cover indicating the title, author, institutional identification, and number in the series. They frequently bear a caveat that the draft is preliminary and intended for discussion, not for publication or quotation. As a working paper, the article is protected against plagiarism, and it can benefit from the editing and comments of the author's friends and colleagues. Not being an official publication, it does not compromise later appearance in a journal. Moreover, the eventual submission may be closer to a publishable form, and the evaluation and editing efforts required by journal editors would diminish. Further savings could accrue if the working papers are submitted in machine-readable form or on tape and if the journal's printer has the appropriate equipment to make use of this technology. Critical reading of working papers by departmental faculty could also provide a more direct evaluation of scholarship for tenure decisions.

Another type of interim dissemination is the use of a central repository that accepts articles (for a fee), evaluates them (for a fee) and makes them available either on demand (reproduced from the author's typescript and advertised through announcements in catalogs and bibliographies) or through blanket offers to any other conventional journal that wishes to publish them. The Philosophy Research Archives at Bowling Green, Ohio, accepts, referees, and publishes on-demand article-length or longer manuscripts in philosophy for a fee. These articles are sold by subscription and by announcement in the *Philosopher's Index*, an annual bibliography. The authors have the freedom to resubmit their articles to some other conventional journal for publication in full-text form. The Archives received 135 manuscripts in 1977, of which 65 were accepted. The demand for these articles has been limited; there were only 85 library subscriptions and requests from only 2 or 3 individuals for each article in 1977. Nevertheless, the large and impressive editorial board of the Archives and rigorous refereeing should make such publications acceptable in tenure decisions. Thus, this procedure recognizes the principle that the author, as beneficiary of the refereeing process, should pay a substantial portion of the cost. Other advantages include elimination of composition costs and perhaps more rapid availability. But these gains are also available through conventional journals.

MICROFORM. The development of micro publishing technology and the increasing availability of machines for reading fiche and printing hard copy of selected pages provides a major supplement to conventional journal publication and an alternative to on-demand publications. It can be less expensive to produce and distribute and much less expensive to store. Moreover, it can improve availability. While user resistance to microforms is high, libraries could find the use of microform journals an attractive alternative to ordering separate articles from marginal journals through interlibrary loans or a national periodicals center.

Microfiche could either be (1) distributed for a small additional charge to regular subscribers who could retain them for reference while disposing of the hard copies after a year or two, or (2) sold separately. Suppose, for example, processing the subscription to this prepackaged set would be minimal or far less than that for the one hundred journals separately. Thus, journals could in effect be bundled as a microform collection and sold to libraries to permit decentralized on-demand publishing where the user can browse the article before printing hard copy. Since microform journals do not compete with paper journals (particularly if the microform set is delayed by a few months) sales of the microform set probably would not noticeably hurt the hard copy library subscriptions of individual journals in the set. The sale of such microfiche collections, if substantial, could generate additional revenues for the individual journals in the set.

The availability of the technology and the feasibility of a bundling scheme do not in themselves point to their substantial use by humanists in the near future. Simple alternatives, such as the use of camera-ready copy and synoptic publishing offer more attractive possibilities.

CONCLUSION

Scholarly journals are not likely to be dislodged from their essential role in the communication of scholarly knowledge. New technology can provide supplementary services. Particularly in the sciences, where there is a higher demand for articles related to well-defined research needs, including commercial ones, the use of on-demand publication and microfilm is likely to increase. But as a means of keeping up with a field, these alternatives cannot supplant the journal. For broad reading, especially in the humanities, the journal is cheaper, more flexible, more efficent in reaching a widely scattered audience—and more comfortable to use. As some humanists put it in the Enquiry's interview study, technology should not intrude on the way that the scholar goes about the conduct of research. Similarly, the various forms of selective and interim publication—though they, too, can be useful—are not substitutes for the traditional journal. Microfiche can help alleviate library storage problems, and after a period of storage in hard copy, conversion of some journals to microfiche may be desirable, but this is an incidental service.

While large journals appear to be capable of self-sufficiency, many small journals face financial difficulty and may not survive unless they enter into some form of cooperative arrangement. Foundation subsidies to encourage joint efforts or consolidation appear desirable, provided that the journals are of high quality or serve a very small readership in an important branch of learning. Some turnover in the journal population is to be expected; weaker journals will cease publication; and innovative scholars will seek to establish new ones. But further growth in the total number of journals in the humanities does not seem needed. What is needed is an improvement in journal management as a link in the network of scholarly communication.

CHAPTER 3

Scholarly Books and Presses

Books published by university presses account for 20 percent of the National Book Awards, 8 percent of the total number of new book titles published annually, and about 1.2 percent of the total sales of the book industry.[1] Compared with their scholarly significance, their national economic importance is trivial. If the university presses were all shut down, the impact on the book trade would be minuscule, and the direct effects on the gross national product would not even be detectable.

It is not money that makes them matter, however; it is the nature of what they publish. University presses are subsidized presses. They were established because of the need to publish meritorious scholarly work that would not attract a large enough readership to warrant publication by commercial publishers. For commercial publishers, most specialized scholarly books would be losing propositions.

If they are to survive and enrich scholarly communication, however, presses must earn their subsidy by serving the scholarly community effectively and by managing their affairs economically and efficiently. These are the considerations underlying the discussion in this chapter.

University presses, of course, do not publish all of the nation's scholarly books. Some of the best learned works appeal to enough general readers to be published by trade publishers. Most textbooks, too, are published commercially because they reach a large market. Indeed, they are the most profitable section of the book business. Moreover, other nonprofit organizations—such as museums, research institutions, and learned

1. J. G. Goellner, "The Future of University Presses," *Library Journal* (September 15, 1978). This highly readable article, written in question-and-answer form, answers the principal questions that are frequently asked about university press operations. Department of Commerce data show that expenditures for printed materials account for about 1 percent of personal consumption; about one-third of this amount is for books and maps. Since 1960, annual book industry sales have hovered around one-fourth of 1 percent of personal consumption expenditures. See J. Kendrick Noble, Jr., "Assessing the Merger Trend," *Publishers Weekly* (July 31, 1978) pp. 39 and 41.

societies—publish monographs and books. Even within many universities there are departments or institutes that conduct their own publishing programs. The U.S. government publishes a vast number of scholarly books and journals and special reports. In short, the world of scholarly publishing is much larger than the domain of the university presses. Nonetheless, the emphasis of this chapter will be on university presses because they publish most of the book-length scholarly work in the humanities and humanistic social sciences, which is the focus of the Enquiry.

Owing to the nature of some of the problems considered here, and the limitations of our data, the discussion will sometimes refer to book publishing in general, sometimes to scholarly publishing, sometimes to university presses, and sometimes to the humanities segment of university press publishing. We will try to leave no doubt in the reader's mind about which aspect of the publishing universe we are talking about, but the reader should be alert to the fact that the focus of the discussion can and will change. The nature of the membership of the Association of American University Presses (AAUP) —which includes ten presses that are not American and four presses that are not affiliated with universities—should be fair warning that the discussion will not be as tidy as one would like it to be.

THE ROLE AND GROWTH OF PRESSES

Time in the world of university presses can be reckoned pre-1949 and post-1949, which was the year in which Chester Kerr published his classic study of university presses. His report provides a benchmark for the measurement of subsequent changes in the field.[2]

The period before 1949 has a literature of its own, marked by the definition and emerging role of scholarly publishing over a period of nearly eighty years. The later period has been characterized first by rapid growth in university publishing and then, during the past decade, the emergence of a number of problems caused by changes in higher education and in the economy. The period since 1949 has been marked, too, by a good deal of research on publishing, such as a report on production problems by Richard G. Underwood, a handbook on university publishing by Gene R. Hawes,

2. Chester Kerr, *A Report on American University Presses,* based on a survey sponsored by the American Council of Learned Societies with a grant from the Rockefeller Foundation (New York, Association of American University Presses, 1949). See also Kerr's update, *American University Publishing 1955: A Supplement to the 'Report on American University Presses* (New York, American Association of University Presses, 1956).

and David Horne's erudite whimsy in the quarterly, *Scholarly Books in America*. The establishment of a journal, *Scholarly Publishing*, by the University of Toronto Press, has provided an indispensable forum for the exchange of ideas among publishers and scholars.[3]

The year 1978, which was the five hundredth anniversary of the world's oldest university publisher—the Oxford University Press—and the one hundredth anniversary of the oldest American press in continuous operation —The Johns Hopkins University Press—provides another benchmark. It is thus a good year to take a fix on the scholarly publishing enterprise.

Both Oxford and Johns Hopkins are members of the AAUP which had seventy-four members at the end of 1978, including ten with their major offices in other countries—Cambridge, Oxford, Edinburgh, British Columbia, McGill-Queens, Laval, Montreal, Toronto, Tokyo, and Universitetsforlaget. Four of the American presses—the Brookings Institution, the Metropolitan Museum, the U.S. Naval Institute, and the Smithsonian Institution—are divisions of distinguished nonprofit research, educational, or cultural organizations that had obtained membership in the association before the bylaws were amended to limit membership to colleges and universities.

The typical university press is a division of a university and is administered by a director, who is an administrative officer of the university; two directors out of five also hold academic rank. Press policies are guided by an editorial board. The acceptance and rejection of manuscripts is based on a carefully organized process of peer review in which scholars from throughout the nation participate.

In 1977 the university presses published 3,999 titles, including paperback reprints of previously published clothbound books, compared with a total of 42,780 titles issued by the American book publishing industry. Sales revenues of the presses totaled $56 million compared with $4.6 billion for the entire book industry. A few presses operate their own printing plants and employ printing staffs.

3. Richard G. Underwood, *Production and Manufacturing Problems of American University Presses* (New York, Association of American University Presses, 1960); and Gene R. Hawes, *To Advance Knowledge* (New York, American University Press Services, 1967). To mark its diamond anniversary in 1961, the University of Toronto Press published an instructive overview, *The University as Publisher*. Herbert S. Bailey, Jr., Director of Princeton University Press, published his book, *The Art and Science of Book Publishing*, commercially (New York, Harper & Row, 1970).

As for the intervening thirty years, the most important elements of the story were summarized by Kerr a decade ago.[4] The 1948–68 period, as he describes it, was clearly a golden era for university presses. Their numbers increased from thirty-five to sixty-nine; the number of employees nearly doubled—rising from 1,725 (including 375 part-time) to more than 3,000, with far fewer than 20 percent working part-time. Professionalism increased in all aspects of university publishing. Book design flourished. In one year, university presses captured seventeen of the fifty Best Book awards of the American Institute of Graphic Arts. There were changes in production technology, too—the shift from letterpress to offset printing, the perfection of glues that made adhesive bindings acceptable for quality paperbacks, and a greater interest in the use of acid-free papers that would ensure longer life for books. Presses also turned increasingly to outside printers. In 1948 eleven presses out of thirty-five owned their own printing plants; in 1968 the figures were eight out of sixty-nine. And instead of asking authors to help defray the cost of books that required a subsidy, presses generally paid royalties. There were also changes in leadership. Two out of five press directors in 1978 had come from commercial publishing, whereas in 1948 most of the directors had entered publishing from the academic world, with only one in eight having commercial publishing experience. Kerr's list of broad developments during this period began with the following comment:

1. American university press publishing has matured. To eagerness has been added substance. To energy, balance. To inclination, experience.
2. With maturity has come identification. The techniques and modes of the "book trade" are important, sure, but even more so are the purposes and being of the university itself. Which is where the university press belongs.[5]

The most recent decade, however, has not been as buoyant. The university presses live in two worlds, the world of book publishing and the world of higher education. For the past ten years, book publishing has been buffeted by the same ups and downs as the rest of the economy, though on balance, the book industry has fared reasonably well. Higher education, however, has encountered rougher going. The slowing of enrollment growth, reduction in federal support for libraries, and budget constraints on every campus have affected the operations of university presses. A few of them shut down and virtually all of them have had to live with financial constraints at one time or another. In addition, from within the network of

4. For a detailed and entertaining account of the 1949–68 period see Chester Kerr, "The Kerr Report Revisited," *Scholarly Publishing* (October, 1969).
5. Ibid.

scholarly communication, the rising expenditures of libraries for periodicals have cut into the unit sales of books. These changes and related developments bear closer scrutiny.

PUBLISHING TRENDS. The proliferation of journals reported in chapter 2 of this report has been accompanied by a similar increase in the number of book titles. The total number of titles published annually in the United States displayed no discernible trend during the first half of the century—hovering around 10,000 titles a year except for slumps in the early 1920s and during the 1930s. During the 1950s, however, the number of new titles published began to rise (see table 3.1) and from 1950 to 1970 it more than tripled. The proliferation of scholarly publication, therefore, was also part of a broader trend reflecting demographic, economic, and educational changes; innovations in publishing also played a role. During the 1970s the rate of growth in the output of all titles slowed down, and the output of university presses, which had risen to 4,130 in 1971, declined for two years. By 1977 it still had not recovered fully. Nevertheless, because far fewer university press titles went out of print during this period than were added, the total number of university press titles in print continued to rise. The total number of books sold rose only slightly, however—about 4 percent for clothbound books, and 10 percent for paperbacks for the 1971–75 period, according to one study.[6] As shown in table 3.2, the result has been a sharp decline in the average number of copies sold per title: paperback sales declined by 44 percent for the commercial publishers and by 25 percent for the university presses included in the sample.

The results are consistent with two assessments:

– Book buyers are being given a wider range of choice.

– Authors and publishers are encountering competition for the book buyer's dollar, and thus an author can expect to sell fewer copies of a new book published today than five years ago.

Here we should reiterate that the figures refer to averages. These data do not show whether the top ten or twenty titles, say, of commercial publishers and university presses are selling fewer copies than the top ten or

6. Fritz Machlup, Kenneth W. Leeson, and associates, *Information Through the Printed Word: The Dissemination of Scholarly, Scientific and Intellectual Knowledge* (New York, New York University, March 15, 1978). This is a preliminary report of a study carried out under grants from the National Science Foundation and the National Endowment for the Humanities, subsequently published in three volumes by Praeger Publishers, Inc. (New York, 1978).

Table 3.1. Output of Book Titles in the United States, for Selected Years, 1950–77

		Selected fields						
Year	All fields	Art	History	Language	Literature	Philosophy, psychology	Religion	Sociology, economics
1950[a]	11,022	357	516	148	591	340	727	515
1960[a]	16,554	470	865	228	736	480	1,104	754
1962	21,901	726	1,212	332	1,097	650	1,455	2,096
1964	28,451	906	1,358	801	1,454	766	1,830	3,272
1966	30,050	1,013	1,619	795	1,812	892	1,809	3,482
1968	30,387	1,117	1,528	502	2,106	946	1,791	4,070
1970[b]	36,071	1,169	1,995	472	3,085	1,280	1,788	5,912
1972	38,053	1,470	1,629	479	2,525	1,164	1,705	6,415
1974	40,846	1,525	1,292	441	2,285	1,368	1,851	6,640
1976[c]	41,698	1,681	2,295	523	1,694	1,386	2,058	6,993
1977	42,780	1,795	2,022	556	1,866	1,372	2,121	6,814

Source: R. R. Bowker Company.

[a] Definitions of disciplinary categories for 1950 and 1960 are not identical with those for subsequent years.

[b] The total number of titles for 1970 rose sharply from 1969 because of (1) the strong growth in the production of hardcover facsimile reprints, (2) a large jump in paperback reprints, and (3) improvements in data gathering.

[c] Beginning with data for 1976, figures on total output are reported in preliminary form for twelve months and in final form after eighteen months to obtain a more comprehensive count that includes books and records that arrive late and that must be compared with Library of Congress data. Library of Congress data exclude some titles by definition. Some publishers do not send their titles to the Library of Congress.

twenty of five years ago or ten years ago. What we may be seeing is a ceiling on the total number of books that the libraries and scholarly readers will buy. The virtual quadrupling of the number of titles published annually over the period 1950–75 and a rapid increase in unit sales was based on a growth rate of book sales that simply was not sustainable. It is not surprising—and no cause for alarm—that the number of copies sold seems to be leveling out, and that further increases in the number of titles published is not likely to lead to an increase in copies sold, at least temporarily.

On the basis of available data it is difficult to determine how much of the leveling off in unit sales is attributable to rising prices, to inferior quality of the additional titles that are being published, to the competition for library funds that has led to a reduction in book purchases, or to a feeling of surfeit among individuals who, after increasing their book purchases over several years, have simply reached a point where they are not willing to buy books at a more rapid rate and, indeed, may be cutting back.

University press directors have been particularly concerned about the decline in unit sales for some years. What is the appropriate response: To increase the number of titles published in order to sustain or increase total unit sales? Or to take a closer look at marginal manuscripts and to turn down manuscripts that have a lower than average potential for sales? Or to continue with their present policies? Most presses have been able to keep their dollar sales rising by increasing their prices to reflect increases in costs. Some have had to raise prices even more rapidly because the decline in the number of copies sold has meant that fixed costs and composition costs have had to be spread over a fewer number of copies. Such higher prices, in turn, run the risk of reducing sales still further as buyers rebel at paying the higher prices. This circular process has discouraging portents.

A separate tabulation prepared for the Enquiry shows the total number of titles in various disciplines published by university presses and other university publishing outlets from 1968 to 1974. Books in the social sciences accounted for most of the growth, increasing by more than 50 percent—from 1,228 titles to 1,881 over the period. The increase in the humanities was about 17 percent, from 857 to 1,003, and in the sciences it was 18 percent. Table 3.3 shows that, as a result of the rapid growth in social science publications, the social sciences displaced the humanities as the major source of new titles published by all university-sponsored organizations.

Sales of university press books in the humanities during the early 1970s present a mixed picture, not noticeably different from that for all university press books. Over the 1971–75 period the number of titles published in each of eight humanistic disciplines rose. Total unit sales rose in four disciplines, declined in three, and were unchanged in one. Sales per title declined in all fields except language and linguistics and art and art history.

ATTITUDES TOWARD SCHOLARLY BOOK PUBLISHING

Judged by replies to the Enquiry's Survey of Scholars in the humanities and humanistic social sciences, scholarly book publishing is meeting the needs of readers and authors, though readers are unhappy about prices and authors want more guidance on how to get their manuscripts published. A separate Enquiry survey of university administrators found solid support for the continued operation of presses, mixed with considerable concern about the large deficits incurred by some presses. In short, if the presses were in trouble at the time of the survey, only insiders seemed aware of the fact.

Table 3.2. Percentage Changes in Book Sales Patterns of a Sample of Publishers from 1971 to 1975

Category	University presses	Commercial publishers
Hardbound books		
Increase in titles in print	24.2	49.5
Change in total copies sold	−7.8	6.2
Change in average number sold per title	−25.7	−29.0
Paperbound books		
Increase in titles in print	43.2	96.9
Change in total copies sold	7.3	10.2
Change in average number sold	−25.1	−44.1

Source: Fritz Machlup, Kenneth W. Leeson and associates, *Information Through the Printed Word: The Dissemination of Scholarly, Scientific and Intellectual Knowledge* (New York, New York University, March 15, 1978) tables 2.6.5 and 2.6.6. Fifteen presses were included in the sample—seven university presses and eight commercial publishers.

Table 3.3. Publication of Scholarly Books by Universities, by Discipline, for Selected Years, 1968–74

Year	Number of titles	Percentage by discipline			
		Humanities	Social sciences	Sciences	Other
1968	3,096	39	31	9	21
1969	3,253	39	31	10	20
1971	3,448	38	34	8	20
1973	3,343	36	33	10	21
1974	4,103	34	40	8	18

Source: Library of Congress data, cited by Robert S. Hohwald, "University Publications in Various Fields," a report for the National Enquiry. Note that the data are for all university sources. University presses account for nearly two-thirds of the titles; university institutes, research libraries, and departments account for the rest.

From the outside, scholarly publishing appeared to be in a healthy state. The source of the problem was not to be found in the quality of the product or service, but in changes in the economic and educational environment and in the managerial response of presses to these altered circumstances.

But if publishers can take heart from the expressions of satisfaction by readers and authors, they will find some cause for concern in the responses to some of the questions asked in the surveys. (Footnote 8 in chapter 2 provides a brief description of the Survey of Scholars.)

SCHOLARS AS READERS.   Humanists are active book readers and book buyers. Nine out of ten respondents to the Survey of Scholars reported reading at least fifty books a year and buying about fifteen. Their estimates of their annual expenditures for books average $150, about twice the amount spent on journals. About 10 percent of the respondents said they read no books, and the same percentage said they generally read four or more books in an average week.

Book reading appears slightly on the increase. Four out of five respondents reported that they were reading as many books as they had read in each of the preceding three years or more. At the most prestigious institutions, respondents reported reading more books than scholars at the least prestigious institutions, but the total amount of time spent reading (journals and books) varied little by type of institution, academic rank, or discipline.

A strong demand for recent titles is apparent. Half the books that were read by respondents had been published in the preceding year or year and a half. Among classicists and philosophers, as might be expected, recent publications are less important than they are among anthropologists and sociologists.

Though they are reading more books, scholars report that they are buying fewer of them. The drop in purchases is slight. A small plurality (38 percent) reported no change in their buying habits, 35 percent reported a decline and 27 percent reported an increase in book buying. Thus, an optimist might stress that two out of three scholars are buying as many books as before, or more. But on the other hand, it is worth noting that whereas 42 percent of the respondents said they were reading more books, only 27 percent said they were buying more, and though only 21 percent said they were *reading* fewer books, 35 percent said they were *buying* fewer (see table 3.4).

The interpretation of these figures is made more difficult by the fact that there are no data to indicate whether the average number of books bought by

Table 3.4. Profile of Scholarly Book Readers
(Percentage of respondents)

A. Change in book-using habits in recent years

	Percentage reporting		
	More	*Fewer*	*Same*
Books read	42	21	37
Books bought	27	35	38
Books borrowed	34	17	49

B. Source of information on latest book bought[a]

Publisher's announcement or catalog	34
Advertisement in scholarly journal	20
Book review	18
Colleague recommendation	15
Citation in article or book	12
Browsing in bookstore	11
Browsing in library	4
Publisher's booth at convention	6

C. Ways of purchasing, ranked in importance

Order from publisher	45
Buy from bookstore shelf	27
Order from bookseller	18
Other	10

Source: National Enquiry Survey of Scholars.
[a] Percentages add up to over 100 because multiple answers were permitted.

respondents in the different groups was the same. Nonetheless, the interpretation that scholars as a group are buying fewer books is consistent with book industry statistics about declines in the number of copies sold. The Survey also shows that one response to rising prices has been to maintain journal subscriptions and reduce book purchases, which was also the typical response by libraries.

Despite the decline in book buying, scholars still depend more heavily on their own purchases than on library borrowing or other sources to obtain current titles. For example, 38 percent reported that they had purchased the latest book they had read, 29 percent said they had borrowed it from the institution's library, and 18 percent said they had received it as a complimentary or review copy.

Scholars buy nearly half their books directly from publishers on the basis of announcements and catalogs supplied by the publisher or from reading advertisements in journals. They rarely see a copy of a book before ordering it, but they are seldom disappointed in what they buy. An overwhelming majority (94 percent) said they would have purchased the book if they had had an opportunity to browse through it before buying. Whether this purchasing pattern should be taken as a reflection of the limitations of book store service or as a tribute to the services provided by publishers cannot be inferred from the data.

The decline in book buying is offset by an increase in library borrowing. Thirty-four percent of the respondents said they had increased the number of books borrowed, and only 17 percent said they had reduced their borrowing.

A substantial majority of scholars (70 percent) agree that most articles and books important to their teaching and research are brought to their attention in a reasonable amount of time. But on this question there is a difference by rank and by discipline. Assistant professors are less satisfied than full professors, and sociologists and anthropologists are much more concerned with the timeliness of information than are classicists and philosophers.

Most scholars consider their personal libraries—which average about 600 volumes and range up to 2,000 volumes—adequate to their needs. But, again, the scholars in lower ranks and at less-prestigious schools tend to be less satisfied.

In general, scholars are satisfied with their access to new material, with the system that brings new books to their attention and delivers them, with the quality of what they buy, and with their own personal library resources.

But this is not to say that they have no complaints. The principal one has already been mentioned: the rapid increase in prices. Asked to select from fifteen problem areas the three that were the most in need of attention, 19 percent of the respondents cited the high price of books, 10 percent cited inadequate university or college library collections, and 9 percent cited too many publications of poor quality. Very few scholars complained about a lack of bibliographic or reference works, or about the problem of deciding what to read. Nor did they express much concern about the delays in publication of books or lateness of book reviews. At the same time, well over half of the respondents (67 percent of assistant professors) said that computer-based bibliographic searches would be useful.

What would scholars be willing to trade in return for lower book prices? Responses to one question indicated that a large majority (86 percent) would accept more paperback editions, and half would accept standardized or less costly design, two changes that they regarded as having only a slight effect on the quality of the publication. However, only 34 percent would accept printing directly from the author's typescript, and only 29 percent would accept lower-quality paper. Clearly unacceptable are savings obtainable from less careful editing (rejected by 95 percent) and reduced author's royalties (rejected by 89 percent).

When the tradeoff was posed in more specific terms, however, the response differed. Readers were asked how they would respond if they were offered a choice between regular publisher's editions of books at full price and a photocopy of the author's original unedited manuscript at a price 30 percent lower. Thirty-nine percent would not buy any books in this form if offered the choice. On the other hand, about the same proportion (41 percent) would be willing to buy some of their books (one-fourth to one-half) in this form, and the remainder (19 percent) would be willing to buy three-fourths to all their books in this form. In other words, three out of five scholarly readers are willing to trade editorial verification and clarification as well as lower-quality production for some books for a substantial reduction in price.

Respondents were also asked to choose among several options for obtaining a $16 book that was unavailable through both their bookstore and library. Two-thirds would request it through interlibrary loan as either a first or second choice. (However, it should be noted that only 2 percent said that they had acquired a copy of the last book they read through interlibrary loan.) Half said they would mail an order to the publisher as a first or second choice. One-fourth said they would use a microfilm version available in their library for use within the library only. With regard to the other options, about equal numbers would give up looking (7 percent) or would place an order with the publisher by phone (9 percent). Both options were preferred over placing an order with a dealer who provides rapid and complete service but charges a $2 fee to do it (4 percent). These responses appear descriptive of current practices, with most users ordering personal copies directly from the publisher or obtaining copies for use (not purchase) through interlibrary loan. The refusal to use a dealer who charges for speedier service may indicate that scholars in the humanities are not compelled by time to pay for special services.

SCHOLARS AS AUTHORS.   Respondents to the Survey of Authors are highly productive scholars. Forty-four percent have published at least one scholarly monograph, and more than 10 percent have published three or more. Productivity varies both by quality of institution and by discipline. At the elite universities, 59 percent of the scholars said they have published one or more scholarly monographs, compared with 25 percent at the least selective universities. By discipline, the responses range from a high of 58 percent for historians to 40 percent for scholars in English, philosophy, Romance languages, and sociology.

Responses also indicate that productivity does not decline markedly in the later stages of a career, suggesting that competition for available publishing opportunities is not likely to diminish over the years. Even though the age structure of the faculty changes, the young scholar a decade or two hence will probably find it no easier to publish than does the young scholar today.

Despite their success in achieving publication, authors have had their failures and their problems in getting their work into print. One of five respondents has given up on the publication of a completed book-length manuscript. The proportion of scholars who have abandoned publication of a manuscript is substantially higher among scholars in the Romance languages than in other fields included in the survey.[7]

On the average, manuscripts that are published have been submitted to two or more publishers. An analysis of responses on publication experience indicates that there is not much difference in the submission records of authors who were previously published and those who were not. Nor is there any measurable difference in acceptance rates among disciplines.

The survey sheds some light on authors' attitudes as well as on their experiences. Most authors believe that there are enough book publishers (as well as enough journals) to enable them to get their work into print. The need is for better information about the publication process rather than an increase in the number of publishing outlets. Since they are readers as well as authors, respondents appear to agree that an increase in quantity, especially if accompanied by a decline in quality, is undesirable, and they seem willing to resist a major expansion of outlets even at the risk of continuing to face difficulties in getting into print. This inference needs to be judged in the light of the fact that the survey sample overrepresents senior and highly productive scholars who have been successful in getting their work published.

7. An Enquiry sample study of manuscripts rejected in 1973 by six university presses shows that by 1977 about one-third had been published after being submitted to an average of four or five publishers. Ten percent of authors responding to the mail survey indicated that they had permanently shelved their manuscripts after submission to a median number of eleven publishers. Manuscripts temporarily shelved totaled 33 percent.

In deciding where to submit their manuscripts, authors give the greatest weight to the publisher's reputation. Of possible reasons for selecting a publisher, 63 percent of the respondents ranked reputation first, followed by likelihood of acceptance, which was ranked first by 23 percent of the respondents. Speed of publication, quality of design and editing, royalties, and promotional effort are minor concerns of roughly equal importance. Among assistant professors and scholars in the lower-status institutions, the factor of probable acceptance was more important.

Overall, the respondents showed considerable satisfaction with book publishing. Their dissatisfaction and proposals for change were directed at journals, as discussed in chapter 2, rather than at presses. But again, there are differences by experience and discipline. Authors who have published two or more books tend to be more critical of promotional and advertising policies of their publishers. Among disciplines, historians (who publish a larger proportion of books per person) put a higher value than do scholars in other disciplines on the speed of book publishing and the need for greater subsidies. Classicists attach a high importance to subsidies and to the need for more lower-priced editions.

UNIVERSITY ADMINISTRATORS. University presses rank high in the estimation of university administrators. An Enquiry survey, by John J. Corson, of senior administrators of universities that have university presses indicates that these institutions are solidly behind their presses.[8] With one or two exceptions, senior officers (president, chancellor, provost, and so forth) staunchly supported their presses even though they were not uniformly optimistic about the financial future of the presses. Most universities were confronted by a period of economic retrenchment at the time of the survey, and some had examined the financial operations of the press. Some had sought to find ways to reduce the institutional subsidies to their presses. Expressions of concern about finances were common among administrators of institutions with the largest press deficits, typically the smaller presses. Administrators of private institutions were more concerned than those of public universities where the public service or regional publishing concept is more pronounced.

Because of financial pressures, a majority of the administrators expressed a willingness to consider the creation of consortia for the purpose of

8. John J. Corson, "The University Press: Prospects for the Future," *Scholarly Publishing* (January 1978). This is a report of a survey of university administrators, conducted for the National Enquiry, April 6, 1977.

carrying on jointly those business functions, such as warehousing and order fulfillment, which do not impinge on their editorial operations or the identity of their university's imprint.

Administrators shared the view of scholars that there is little need for additional presses. Responses from some fifteen research-oriented universities, which have no active presses, indicated that operating cost is the principal deterrent, followed by the general opinion that these institutions seem to be served adequately by existing presses. In a few state institutions new cooperative ventures, with other public institutions within the state, were considered to be possibilities.

THE PROBLEMS OF THE PRESSES

The predicament of university presses is a strange one. They have satisfied their major constituencies—the authors, the readers, and the university administrators—but for most of them the goals of financial stability and financial security are as elusive as ever. To a large extent, their difficulties arise from pressures outside their control: the increasing number of publishers and the number of book titles being published, the higher costs that must be passed along in the form of increased prices, the leveling off in college enrollments, and constraints on university budgets, particularly library budgets. Competition has increased in recent years both for good manuscripts and for buyers. Since no lessening of most of these pressures is likely during the next few years, the presses must learn to cope with them by improving their efficiency, by developing new markets, and by developing a rationale for subsidies.

In principle, the case for subsidizing scholarly communication is undeniable. In practice, however, the size of subsidies and the selection of recipients must be decided on a basis that makes sense to donors as well as to scholars and presses. The first requirement is for presses to demonstrate that they are using their resources efficiently and imaginatively. Several aspects of their operations bear examination.

SIZE AND EFFICIENCY.   One conclusion emerges strongly from an examination of the operating statistics published annually for members of the AAUP: Costs of production and overhead expenses vary enormously, and much of the variation can be explained by size. The presses that are able to break even (after title subsidies) are primarily the largest presses. Warehousing and shipping costs tend to be lower per unit for larger operations, and overhead expenses as a proportion of net sales also tend to be lower (see table 3.5.)

Table 3.5. *Illustrative Operating Data on University Presses*

Category	All presses		Net sales up to $250,000		Net sales above $1 million	
	Percentage of net sales		Percentage of net sales		Percentage of net sales	
	Average	Mid-range	Average	Mid-range	Average	Mid-range
Cost of sales	51	44–56	61	45–69	51	44–53
Gross margin on sales	48	43–55	38	30–54	48	46–55
Operating expenses	63	60–101	115.	88–145	56	52–62
Editorial	9	8–14	16	10–20	8	7–9
Production	3	3–7	10	6–11	2	2–4
Marketing	17	15–25	27	22–35	16	14–19
Fulfillment	13	11–19	18	13–21	11	9–14
General and administrative	19	60–101	42	28–67	17	14–19
Net income (or loss)	(11)	(2–57)	(75)	(56-109)	(5)	2–(11)

Note: Figures may not add to totals because of rounding. (Mid-range is the range of the middle 50 percent of the presses, that is, excluding the top and bottom quartiles.)

Source: Data selected from 1977 *University Press Statistics*, table 12, prepared for the AAP and AUPS by John P. Dessauer, Inc. Reproduced with permission.

Drawing valid conclusions about efficiency from statistics on press operations is difficult because accounting practices differ from press to press, despite progress in recent years toward uniformity. Thus, while any member press of the AAUP can gain a great deal of useful information by comparing its financial statements with the annual publication of press-operating statistics issued by the AAUP, it is difficult for an observer to make generalizations with confidence. Moreover, while comparisons by size are interesting, no inferences about the efficiency of any single press should be made on the basis of size alone. Large presses, as well as small ones, have encountered serious financial problems in recent years, and some of the best-managed small and medium-sized presses may be outperforming some of their larger competitors. Nonetheless, it is clear that deficits (after title subsidies) are relatively much higher for the smallest presses. Deficits average 75 percent of net sales for presses with sales up to $250,000 compared with an average of 11 percent for all presses. The mid-range of these presses (which excludes the highest and lowest 25 percent of the sample) shows deficits ranging from 56 percent to 109 percent of net sales.

Thus, one in four of the smallest presses has deficits at least equal to the size of net sales. The differences in general and administrative expenses are also very striking.

The data in table 3.5 provide a starting point, but we know of no simple rule of thumb that will enable a university administrator or press director to determine whether a press is of a viable size or is being operated at maximum efficiency. We can, however, suggest a way of thinking about the problem that a university might employ. This line of reasoning leads not to a press or no-press alternative, but rather to consideration of a number of changes in the way presses can be run.

We begin by distinguishing between those functions, on the one hand, that are the central publishing functions—the manuscript selection and dissemination decisions—and, on the other hand, the performance of certain tasks to implement those decisions—tasks that are vital to the publishing operation but that can be contracted out to others.

The design of a book, for example, has long been considered an important publishing decision both for esthetic and economic reasons, but once the design has been approved, any qualified printer can carry it out subject to the publisher's review. Thus, while it was once customary for many publishers, commercial and university alike, to own their own printing plant, this is now a rarity (about one in ten among university presses). Indeed, many publishers obtain their book designs from free-lance graphic artists.

Similarly, pricing decisions and advertising and promotion policies fall within the essential responsibilities of the publisher, but the layout and placement of space advertising may be easily farmed out. Some direct mail campaigns can also be handled outside, subject to press supervision. The processing of orders, billing, warehousing, and shipping are all functions that can be assigned to others.

The essential question for a press director is whether any of the functions currently being performed by the press itself can be handled more efficiently and more economically by an alternative service—either by a commercial firm or by another university press or group of presses. We see no reason why a press should continue to carry out support functions that can be provided more efficiently by others. If no alternative service is available, a press should investigate the possibilities of achieving economies and better service by joining with one or more additional presses to form a consortium.

For any number of reasons, a university may decide that it would prefer to pay an additional subsidy to maintain full control over all press functions, including billing and so on. The cost of doing so might not be great. Despite the gap in performance that appears in a comparison based on percentages, the dollar amount may be rather small. Nonetheless, the press ought at least to make an effort to determine the real magnitude of the subsidy it is given. It should also recognize that its claim for subsidies is weakened by a deliberate decision to operate at a less efficient level than other presses.

OVERPRINTING, UNDERPRICING, AND INVENTORY VALUATION. It would be a mistake to put too much stress on the dramatic effect of size on efficiency. Quite independent of the size of a press is the quality of the management's decisions on the number of copies to print, the price, and the valuation of inventory. Overprinting and underpricing, in particular, can be disastrous to a press. Both result from the same fallacious reasoning. Because the unit cost of a book declines with an increase in the number of copies printed (since composition costs and fixed costs are spread over more books), presses have been tempted to print large editions in order to justify lower prices.[9] For most scholarly books, however, a modest reduction in price by a couple of dollars is not likely to increase sales, and presses that increase the quantity printed in order to justify a lower price often end up with warehouses full of unsalable books. A much more realistic approach is to determine the print run on the basis of such factors as sales of similar books and to set the price on the basis of costs tempered by an understanding of what the market will accept. If this calculation, after careful reconsideration, shows clearly that the book will not pay its way, it is better to recognize that fact at the outset and either seek a subsidy or take the loss. The alternative of overprinting and underpricing merely results in self deception and in a larger loss in the future—larger because more books will have been printed and less revenue will be captured by each book that is sold.

Closely related to these problems is the overvaluation of inventory. Carrying inventory at a value far in excess of the market value can lead presses to misjudge their financial position. Presses need to follow a conservative policy that fully writes off the value of overstock within five years after printing. This practice is especially important as a check against perpetuating the mistakes of overprinting. Moreover, during a period of

9. Nazir A. Bhagat and Robert A. Forrest, "How Many Copies Should We Print?" *Scholarly Publishing* (October 1977). An Enquiry study of a sample of six university presses, cited here, shows that half the books in their warehouses would not be sold in the next five years after the survey was taken. One press had sufficient inventory of 20 percent of the titles in the sample to last for a century at the current rate of sale.

inflation presses must reprice the books in the inventory. Otherwise, as one consultant puts it, "Sales from the backlist recover yesteryear's deflated dollars to pay for today's inflated costs."[10]

The importance of these and other managerial decisions underscores the need for better financial analysis and financial planning by presses and a better understanding of press operations by university administrators. In varying degrees of sophistication, presses of all sizes keep records of sales, production costs, inventory, accounts receivable, accounts payable, and a mixture of miscellaneous reports. But not all of them follow the recommended format for the operating statement, which is the key financial statement. The fundamentals and framework of the financial system, however, are the same for small, medium, and large presses. Thus, presses that follow the standard format will not only facilitate comparisons of their operations with those of other presses, but will also facilitate the improvement of industry statistics. A proper operating statement, coupled with competent financial forecasts, can also help the university understand that over and above the annual operating subsidy the press needs a continued commitment of support and working capital for financing salable inventory and of accounts receivable.

OPPORTUNITIES FOR COLLABORATION. In chapter 2 we presented the case for consolidation of journal operations. We believe that in book publishing the case is equally strong for collaboration, which may take many forms. From the standpoint of simplicity, the purchase of services from an established press is the most attractive form of collaboration. It also may be the most advantageous financially, since costs can be estimated with some confidence in advance, and no capital investment may be necessary. Moreover, there should be little uncertainty about the quality of service.

Some members of the Association of American University Presses have taken the lead in providing such services—*clustering* is the term used by J. G. Goellner, director of The Johns Hopkins University Press, and others. Johns Hopkins (with total revenues of nearly $3 million), for example, tailors its services to the needs of the collaborating organization. It handles five tasks—order processing, credit management, data processing, ware-

10. Personal communication from Jack Schulman, publishing consultant and former director of the Cambridge University Press. This discussion of overprinting and underpricing is based on Mr. Schulman's memo to the National Enquiry.

housing, and shipping—for the SUNY Press. For the University of Pennsylvania Press, which processes its own orders, Johns Hopkins provides data processing, shipping, and warehousing. For the University Press of Virginia, which handles its own order processing and warehousing, Johns Hopkins provides computer services; telephone transmission enables the computer in Baltimore to print invoices, statements, sales analyses, and periodic reports at a terminal in Virginia's Charlottesville offices.

An alternative to purchasing services is that of forming a consortium to provide them cooperatively. Several neighboring small presses that are not near a large press or commercial source may try to work out a joint plan for billing, warehousing, and shipping from a central point that is more efficient and less costly than any press can provide by itself. Establishing a new organization may be more difficult than buying services from an existing one. Agreement on policies and procedures will require the approval of several different universities, and additional capital may be needed to launch the operation. Loans from the parent university may be needed, or perhaps a grant from a foundation can be obtained if the evidence is clear that the consortium can succeed in bringing the presses closer to a break-even point. Offsetting these obstacles is the opportunity to participate in the management of the consortium, which might be important to some press directors. Both the consortium and the purchase of services add an element of risk that is not present in the do-it-yourself operation. The press participating in a cooperative arrangement must live with the understanding that the services it buys or shares could be discontinued for reasons that are unrelated to its own performance.

Nevertheless, despite these added difficulties, collaboration does work. Harvard and M.I.T. have successfully established a joint warehouse. For the sale of books abroad, California, Cornell, and Johns Hopkins have established a marketing organization in London, the International Book Export Group (IBEG). Columbia and Princeton have a joint office in England and so do Chicago, Harvard, and M.I.T. The American University Press Group in London represents eleven publishers: Alabama, Brigham Young, Illinois, Indiana, Missouri, Nebraska, Notre Dame, Penn State, Texas, Washington, and Wisconsin. These consortia have lasted long enough and succeeded well enough to confirm the view that the consortium is a workable form of organization.

An alternative to cooperation is the merger of several presses into a single organization. So far, the university presses have escaped the merger wave that has engulfed many trade publishers, but they are not immune to the pressures that made mergers look attractive to commercial publishers. The response of some universities in New England is instructive. Although it was not formed by a merger of several existing presses, but rather as an entirely new press, the University Press of New England exemplifies how several institutions can collaborate in a joint venture. For several years Brandeis University, Clark University, Dartmouth College, the University of New Hampshire, the University of Rhode Island, and the University of Vermont have carried on a joint publishing venture, headed by a director operating out of Hanover, New Hampshire. The experience of this press suggests that some small presses, with geographic proximity or with complementary lists, may find merger a more attractive alternative than a consortium. The foregoing discussion points to the following recommendation.

Recommendation 3.1.   Collaboration in fulfillment
Scholarly presses should collaborate in the management of fulfillment and data processing operations. The economies of scale achieved through computerization and mechanization can be especially great for small presses, those with annual sales of about $500,000 or less— which comprise nearly half of the AAUP membership. One way to reduce costs is to buy services from larger presses. Another is to form a consortium—a more difficult solution than buying services from an established press, but one that is feasible. Merger is a third possibility if collaboration and consolidation seem desirable for the entire range of press functions.

Collaboration within a university also needs to be considered. Purchases of word processors and copying or printing equipment should be coordinated to prevent unnecessary duplication and to take advantage of more advanced technology. A group of units within a university may be able to purchase much more efficient equipment than could a single division. On some campuses, it may be possible for an established press to provide warehousing or data processing services for other institutes and divisions that have their own publishing operations. Consolidation of publishing operations may prove advantageous on some campuses. It is also possible that a comparative study would show that the cost of using on-campus facilities is much greater than the cost of publishing in cooperation with learned societies or commercial publishers specializing in technical and scholarly books for limited audiences (such as Academic Press, Ballinger, Westview Press, Lexington Books, Sage Publications, and so on).

Further opportunities for collaboration lie in the area where they have been most widely developed—in the program conducted by the AAUP on behalf of all member presses. The association, formally organized in 1946 after twenty-odd years of informal gatherings of press directors, has played a strong supporting role in the development of scholarly publishing. Over the years it has helped set standards of quality for press operations, conducted studies of press activities, operated joint book exhibits, developed the Educational Directory mailing list, promoted the compilation of press operating statistics, and provided for the systematic exchange of information and ideas among members at its annual meetings.[11]

One of its achievements was the quarterly publication of *Scholarly Books in America (SBA)*, founded in 1953 and distributed without charge for more than a decade to a quarter million scholars and libraries throughout the world. It printed brief descriptions of new books and brief articles, serious and humorous, on problems of authorship and publishing. Its revival by the AAUP not only would help promote book sales, but would also promote a better understanding of the world of scholarly publishing—a need that is documented in the Enquiry's Survey of Scholars.

The *SBA,* which was financed by a charge imposed on each title listed in the publication, died because several large presses dropped out, preferring to concentrate their funds on their own promotion. But as our study indicates, subject matter catalogs covering all university presses can be immensely useful to buyers, especially those overseas. They are of special benefit to smaller presses that cannot afford global direct mail promotion. Among worthwhile projects for the AAUP, included in the recommendation below, would be a study of alternative ways to publish and to finance either a new *SBA* or a program of subject matter catalogs.

Recommendation 3.2. The role of the AAUP

The AAUP, acting on behalf of its membership of seventy-four presses and nonprofit organizations, should give high priority to projects of mutual interest. These include the issuance of subject field catalogs, the revival of the cooperative quarterly *Scholarly Books in America (SBA)*, the monitoring of developments in technology and in the field of

11. The Association of American University Presses is located at One Park Avenue, New York, N.Y. 10016. Membership is limited to publishers that meet a number of eligibility criteria.

copyright, improvements in operating statistics (no data are yet provided on journals published by presses), and assistance to presses planning collaborative efforts. Historically, foundation grants have been important in initiating efforts that have later become self-sustaining, such as the Educational Directory, and such grants may be warranted in the future to help launch projects that can benefit presses in general.

MULTIPLE-TRACK PUBLISHING. Most scholars and publishers agree that not all competent research should be published in books and journals—either because (1) the number of readers is too small or the shelf life too short to warrant the cost of publishing, or (2) because the material need be accessible only for reference purposes by microform or computer printouts.

In a provocative paper written for the Enquiry, August Frugé developed the distinction between "publishing" and "recording."[12] What is needed, in his view, is a two-track system. One track is for traditional publishing in much the form in which it operates now, characterized by rigorous selectivity and vigorous marketing efforts that seek to bring a book to the attention of those who might be interested in it. The other track is for recording and making available through a centralized bibliographic service lesser works that may be useful sometimes but that do not merit publication. Frugé believes that only through such a two-track system can publishing, as it is practiced today, be protected from engulfment by the proliferation of research studies. And only by offering the second-track alternative—recording—can scholars be prevented from wasting their time duplicating work that has already been done and be assured access to the full range of knowledge in their field. All competent scholarly work would find a place in the system, but not all would be published.

The handmaidens of the recording system are a bibliographic system that is universal and easily accessible, supplemented by a delivery system that may range from a video screen to a printer that copies a study "on demand," that is, a device capable of making a so-called hard copy from the microform image in which the information is stored.

The management of the recording system envisioned by Frugé would be decentralized. Universities and other organizations throughout the coun-

12. August Frugé, "Beyond Publishing: A System of Scholarly Writing and Reading," *Scholarly Publishing* (pt. 1, July 1978; and pt. 2, October 1978).

try could administer entry of manuscripts into the system (for a fee roughly equivalent to the cost of performing this task) and access to the material in the system (for a fee covering the cost of this service).

The workability and desirability of the two-track approach depend on several factors, including the views of authors, the views of faculty committees responsible for promotion and tenure decisions, and the usefulness of the material to readers.

The Enquiry's Survey of Scholars suggests that authors are willing to consider alternative modes of publication so long as the form of the product—conventional books, on-demand publications, and so on—does not by itself prejudice a faculty committee's assessment of the completed research. But since recording is avowedly different from publication, its acceptance by scholars concerned with career advancement would depend on the willingness of faculty committees to abandon formal publication as a major criterion of evaluation. Frugé argues persuasively what many others also believe strongly—that scholars should be judged on the quality of completed research rather than on its publication, since publishability of a manuscript often depends on the probable size of the readership and the cost of production, matters that are irrelevant to the quality of scholarship.

If faculty and university administrators were generally willing to base their evaluations solely on their own reading of scholarly papers, the distinction between recording and the publication for purposes of evaluation would be erased. At the same time, the case for establishing a recording system would be also greatly reduced. If publication were no longer essential to career advancement, the pressure to publish would be reduced—which, in turn, would lessen the incentive to start new journals and publish more monographs. A manuscript would suffice.

In short, a change in the criteria for assessing faculty performance could have an enormous impact, and it is this issue, rather than the two-track system, that is the crux of the matter.

Apart from the relationship of publication and recording to the success of an academic career is the role of recording in the promotion of scholarly communication. Whether it would help would depend on the merit of what is recorded. Frugé recognizes that quality control is one essential step in establishing the system. Not everything would be recorded—only those manuscripts that were sponsored by a university, learned society, or other appropriate group.

That his proposed procedure would provide an adequate safeguard seems questionable, however. At some points of entry, barriers to poor or trivial work may be effective. In others it would not, and "quickie" recording points would become rapidly known. Pressures for inclusion are likely to dominate. Since there is no practical limit on the capacity of the system, there is no real incentive to exercise restraint. Admission to the system would be virtually costless to those who administer it, but the cost of serious refereeing by a sponsor would be substantial both in time and effort. In the long run, the reputation of recorded material is likely to decline, lessening the usefulness of the system.

Our views, like Frugé's, are conjectural. But it is also worth noting that the scholarly community is divided between those who think too much is being published and those who, unable to get their work published, think that publication opportunities are inadequate. So long as publication is a criterion for advancement, there will be pressures to increase outlets for publication. But, interestingly, there seem to be no comparable complaints among humanists that there is too little material to read. Already they are inundated and seek better access to what has been published. Though there is always room for something better, there is no dearth of material to read, and we fear that the second track invites the preservation of a great deal of undigested, ephemeral, and not very useful material that might otherwise be mercifully lost; this accretion will be a dubious contribution to the system of scholarly communication. Horace's advice to writers, that more should be scratched out than retained, might well be pondered for lesser works of scholarship: more, perhaps, should be forgotten than preserved.

The two-track proposal, while it does not offer a solution, nevertheless makes a notable contribution to the discussion of the dilemma proposed by pressures to publish and the growth in the production of manuscripts.

Another informative taxonomy, similar to one developed by Robert W. Funk, the founder of Scholars Press, is the following five-level classification.[13] It covers the varieties of communication from informal exchanges among scholars to the embodiment of tested scholarship in works of reference.

1. *Informal communications, primarily the exchange of papers prepared for seminars and annual meetings or working papers presenting preliminary results of research in progress.* These communications, which are intended primarily to develop and test ideas, are becoming increasingly

---

13. Robert W. Funk, "Issues in Scholarly Publishing," *Scholarly Publishing* (October 1977). This is Part 1 of a two-part series critical of university press publishing and supportive of the role of other kinds of scholarly publishing agencies, especially those serving learned societies.

important because of delays in the publication of journal articles and the availability on campus of efficient means of duplication. Another type of communication, although different in character, can be put in this category—the so-called marginalia consisting of the notes and comments that appear in journals or newsletters.

2. *Materials that have current and archival value but do not need to be refereed. These include proceedings of symposia and conferences, teaching materials, and concordances.* By and large, this material usually does not justify rigorous evaluation and peer review, but it may warrant indexing in a bibliographic system. Some of it may be printed and distributed by learned societies to their members. Dissertations also probably belong in this category. Currently, in the humanities, there exists no uniform means of recording, storing, and indexing these materials, except for dissertations. A model for recording miscellaneous scholarly material does exist in education: ERIC, Educational Resources Information Center. Whether it could be adapted to the humanities and the humanistic social sciences at a reasonable cost that scholars and libraries would be willing to pay is not clear. ERIC has been in operation for about a decade and adds to its huge bank of information upwards of 20,000 items annually, which are screened, indexed, and made accessible on demand in hard copy or microform.

3. *Monographs that are published in very small quantities, or as needed. (On-demand, on-request, access,* and *passive* are terms used to define this kind of publishing; yet none is appropriately descriptive. Perhaps a more appropriate term will be coined.) Here would be captured works of quality and significance, for which the expected use is too small or uncertain to warrant conventional publishing. Screening, refereeing, and reviewing would be rigorous, and would certify the work for purposes of promotion and tenure. These publications would be copyrighted and cataloged like other monographs, but would be given less editing, design, and manufacturing attention than conventional books and generally would be promoted selectively to specialized markets.

4. *Conventional books or monographs and journals.* These are the works of scholarship that are refereed and printed, promoted and distributed to wider audiences by traditional publishers, commercial or nonprofit.

5. *Reference works and research and bibliographic tools, including consolidated bibliographic systems and computerized data bases.* For reasons of efficiency and comprehensiveness, such data bases need to be

compatible with others and integrated with the output of materials in categories 2, 3, or 4.

Scholarly writing placed initially into category 2 or 3 need not be limited to that category for the duration of its useful life. A study that is entered originally into an on-demand system might later be judged by scholars or editors to be deserving of a larger readership. Similarly, a work of uncertain demand originally published in a very small quantity in category 3 might, on the basis of scholarly interest, be republished conventionally. The Scholars Press, for example, has had considerable success in publishing dissertations in some classical disciplines that have cooperated in imposing higher writing standards. Print runs range from several hundred to several thousand. Composition is standardized, and costs are kept low so that the selling price can be kept at the level of quality paperbacks. A market for dissertations at this price and in the selected disciplines has been developed among individual scholars.

The first three tiers of communication contain a great deal of material that is not of interest to conventional publishers, but which is of considerable importance to scholars and learned societies. In disciplines where the market for specialized works is too small to interest conventional publishers, learned societies have established publishing programs of their own. The Scholars Press serves 20,000 scholars representing four learned societies and a dozen institutions in religion and language. Subsidies, in the form of contributed time by society members and economies in production have contributed to the growth of the press. As scholars began to move into the publishing world, they learned that "the fact of publication became more important than the physical form. . . . As publishers, scholars came voluntarily to the more economic practices they had resisted as authors."[14]

This review of the types of scholarly communication provides a useful reminder of the point made at the beginning of this chapter, that the university press is only one segment of the scholarly communication network. For several decades the press has played a dominant role in the publication of monographs, journals, and books in the humanities. As the foregoing discussion makes clear, however, a great deal of other important scholarly communication takes place, particularly under the auspices of the learned

14. Ibid.

societies and of scholars who independently duplicate and distribute their articles before publication.

There is room enough in the scholarly world for a variety of participants in the communication process.[15] Challenges to established ways of doing things reflect vitality as well as understandable sources of friction. There is a case perhaps for maintaining a distinction between traditional publishing and other modes of producing and disseminating articles and books, but at the same time the learned societies that succeed in publishing highly specialized monographs written by their members may build up sufficient loyalty to be given manuscripts with broader appeal, a step that would lead to the blurring of the distinction. One reconciliation between presses and learned societies would be the publication of books under a joint imprint of the press and the learned society, similar to the proposal discussed for the publication of works sponsored by other universities, or the arrangements whereby many presses now publish on behalf of museums, research institutions, and other organizations.

The role of on-demand service for books has been debated vigorously in recent years, ever since technological advances made it possible to print books one copy at a time at a reasonable price.[16] Its backers say the on-demand approach offers an alternative way of publishing manuscripts not being published in conventional editions.

On-demand has proved its utility for some purposes, as indicated in chapter 2. The storage of journals and books in microfilm, and their duplication either in microfiche or in hard copy at a price of a few cents a page, means that no book need go out of print. This service provides an enormous advantage for scholarship, eases the storage problems of libraries, and relieves scholarly publishers of the responsibility for trying to keep in print journals and books for which there is too little demand to warrant the cost of storage and of tying up capital.

The usefulness of a second role has also been demonstrated. The operation of University Microfilms, with Dissertation Abstracts as a buying guide, has assured the availability of doctoral research without imposing a burden on scholarly publishing.

15. J. G. Goellner, "The Ant and the Aphid," *Scholarly Publishing* (January 1978). This is a university press director's comment on the issues raised by Funk. The second part of the Funk statement appears in the same issue.

16. For two contrasting views of the role of on-demand publishing, see Herbert S. Bailey, Jr., "The Limits of On-Demand Publishing," *Scholarly Publishing* (July 1975); and Datus C. Smith, Jr., "A Case for On-Demand Publishing," *Scholarly Publishing* (January 1976). Mr. Bailey is the director of the Princeton University Press and Mr. Smith a former director. See also Frugé. "Beyond Publishing," discussed above.

The controversy lies in another area: Is on-demand really an alternative form of publishing, just a useful printing device, or merely an additional library service? Debates on this issue have not been sufficiently decisive to answer the question about the future role of on-demand publishing. Nor is there any reason to provide a definitive answer here. The issue will be decided not by logic but by the marketplace. Experiments will continue. University Microfilms, for example, has gone beyond the on-demand service for dissertations to develop two complementary services for monographs, an Imprint Series and a Sponsor Series.[17]

THE QUESTION OF QUALITY AND PRODUCTION STANDARDS. Scholarly books are generally the products of long periods of gestation, and they are expected to enjoy a long life. They are intended to be works of greater durability than the average publication, which argues for greater attention to details of accuracy, nuance, clarity, esthetics, and permanence. Those are qualities that scholars themselves rate highly—but not qualities to be purchased at any price.

Publishing decisions regarding every book require a balancing of conflicting requirements, especially of cost and quality. Editors need enough time to be reasonably sure that the manuscript has succeeded fully in conveying the intended meaning. Designers need to feel reasonably free to draw on the rich resources of printing technology to create pleasing images that will also enhance the readability of what is printed. Printers aspire to maintain the highest standards of craftsmanship. But between the finest work and the most casually written and most cheaply duplicated pages lies a vast range of possibility. Even though convention has narrowed the range for what is acceptable for certain classes of publication, the opportunities for tradeoffs remain great between the ideal and the least expensive as publishers seek to determine the point at which further investment in quality leads to price increases that reduce sales.

17. A university or learned society that wishes to participate in the Imprint Series assumes full editorial responsibility for the publication, provides University Microfilms with camera-ready copy, and authorizes use of its imprint; University Microfilms handles production, storage, and fulfillment. To publish a work in the Sponsor series, an author finds an organization that is willing to state that a study merits publication and then pays University Microfilms to put the title into the system. Buyers pay to obtain the copy on-demand. Carrollton Press, Inc., of Arlington, Virginia, embarked on a similar monograph publishing operation in 1979. It offers universities and associations the opportunity of publishing titles under their own imprint in limited editions of fifty copies or more, supplemented by an on-demand service. It promises limited promotional services and requires no subsidy. Authors must provide camera-ready copy.

Most questions of cost and quality lie outside the agenda on which we have focused our attention. But two are near the center of our concerns: one is the durability of books, and the other is the size of books.

The availability of cheap paper has been very useful in furthering written communication of all kinds. Much that is put down on paper has served its purpose in a few days, months, or years, and its permanence is of little consequence. But material intended for useful life measured in decades or centuries is ill served if it is printed on paper that crumbles and encased in covers and bindings that do not hold. Libraries which have seen a growing proportion of their book funds go into the repair or repurchase of important books have become increasingly concerned about the durability of what they buy.

For the average university press title, libraries account for about half the total sales. Thus, presses should be especially sensitive to this problem and are in a particularly advantageous position to meet the libraries' requirements. Most university press books are short-run books; that is, they are printed in editions ranging from a few hundred to a few thousand. For such editions, the cost of paper, compared with the cost of composition and printing, is relatively low; for commercial publishers, printing in editions of tens of thousands, the cost of paper is relatively much more important. Thus the costs of university press books will be little affected by the requirement that they be printed on acid-free stock, while the benefits of their doing so are very great for their principal customers. The need for commercial publishers to take into account the shelf life of their products is equally great from the library's point of view, but since libraries constitute a relatively smaller proportion of the market for books of general interest, commercial publishers may argue that it does not make much sense to spend more money on durable paper for all books since only a relative few are expected to last a long time and be heavily used. (The difference in the library and publisher interest on this question of durability has led to proposals for the licensing of special library editions of work produced to meet library specifications and sold exclusively to libraries.)[18]

The proliferation of books has caused librarians to become especially concerned about storage space. Not only are more books being produced now than were ten or twenty years ago, but they are being produced in larger

---

18. See Herbert S. Bailey, Jr., "The Traditional Book in the Electronic Age," Fifth of the R. R. Bowker Memorial Lecture Series, Nov. 10, 1977 (New York, Bowker, 1978).

sizes. Partly to make books appear more impressive and worth the higher prices that have had to be charged during a period of inflation, some publishers have been issuing many hardbound titles in larger formats and printed on bulking papers that may fatten a book by 25 percent or more. Libraries can buy more books if they have space to store them and do not have to divert funds to provide shelving or new buildings. A commitment by the publishing industry to thinner books would be directly translatable into a reduction in the demand for library construction. For university presses, the major need is a commitment to durability, as indicated below.

Recommendation 3.3.   Production standards
Scholarly books should be printed on "permanent/durable" opaque paper and bound in cloth with sewn bindings. To encourage the acceptance of these quality standards, foundations that subsidize publications should insist on the use of acid-free and durable papers and sturdy bindings as a condition of their grants.

OTHER ISSUES: SPECIALIZATION, JOURNALS, GOVERNING BOARDS, AND MULTIPLE SUBMISSIONS.   Several other questions related to university press operations bear mention, though not extended discussion. They are matters on which there is little disagreement among press directors but which are not as well understood by others concerned with press operations.

Specialization.   No American scholarly press is large enough to publish effectively in all disciplines. A press in a large university may be under pressure from thirty or forty departments to publish in their fields. Politically, since the press is supported by and is intended to serve the university, it is difficult to resist these pressures, especially when works of undoubted quality are offered. But the press may have the capacity to publish only thirty to fifty books per year, and if it publishes only one or two titles a year in a field, it cannot market them efficiently. Roughly, a press can have ten specialties if it publishes fifty books a year, or six if it publishes thirty. It should plan and, on the average, publish about five books per year in each field in which it specializes. The fields of specialization must be carefully chosen by the staff and the board of the press, keeping in mind the strengths of the university and the press's previous performance.

By specializing in this way, press editors can become expert in the fields selected. They can concentrate their list-building efforts and make better choices. Specialization will also help scholars to know where to submit their manuscripts and where to look for new titles to add to their private libraries. It will permit the presses to focus their promotion and to issue regular subject catalogs.

Recommendation 3.4. Specialization

A press should specialize in selected subject fields and make known to authors and buyers the subjects in which it maintains publishing programs.

Journals.   University presses have had mixed experiences in the publication of journals. Journals have contributed to the strength of some presses and have required substantial subsidies from others. Several large presses, such as California, Chicago, and Johns Hopkins, have established fairly autonomous journal divisions that are expected to break even on their operations and complement their book publishing operations. At the other extreme, some presses have in recent years found journals to be costly and have divested themselves of those that were not paying their way. In general, the experience of university presses bears out the comments on economies of scale discussed in chapter 2.

In some circumstances it may be advantageous for a press to publish fewer than four or five journals. If the journals are closely tied to the book publishing program, the press may benefit by acquiring excellent monographs as a result of the journal connection. There also may be promotional advantages flowing from the tie-in. However, the publication of only a few journals of small circulation is not likely to be efficient either for the presses or the journals.

Recommendation 3.5.   Presses and journals

We recommend that presses publishing only a few journals consider transferring them to other publishers or acquire additional journals if economies can thereby be achieved. We do not suggest an arbitrary minimum, but urge only that the costs and advantages of journal publication be carefully considered to determine whether the journal operation strengthens or weakens the press. Further, for the benefit of presses publishing journals, the AAUP should include data on journals in their statistical studies.

Governing boards.   The relationship of the press to its parent university is of crucial importance. Questions of press autonomy and responsibility, and the amount of financial support it should receive are approached differently by different institutions. As part of the overall financial appraisal that has been taking place throughout higher education in recent years, universities have been scrutinizing the costs of operating their presses. The survey of administrators discussed earlier in this chapter indicated that sponsoring institutions are generally requiring their presses to be more cost conscious, efficient, and flexible.

In a quest for greater managerial efficiency and institutional responsibility, the role of the board of directors or board of governors of the press calls for particular attention. The board is generally appointed by the president of the university (or provost or chancellor) and shares responsibility for determining the size and scope of the publishing program.

Representation on the board is usually divided among three groups: the faculty, the university administration (including the press director), and outsiders—mostly publishers, lawyers, or businessmen (usually alumni). The board chairman is sometimes selected from among the outsiders and the vice chairman from either the faculty or the administration.

A board thus organized, and meeting at least twice a year, is able to give the press director the advantage of discussions reflecting a wide range of viewpoints. It provides an ongoing forum for testing proposed policy changes or the need for reconsideration of existing policies. It prevents the imposition of a narrow viewpoint by a director, an administration official, or faculty member. It improves communication between the press and faculty. Indeed, its mere existence helps increase the confidence of the rest of the campus and alumni in the entire enterprise.

Recommendation 3.6. Role of the board

University administrators and press directors who have not considered the role of their board in recent years should review the responsibilities and performance of the board to make sure that it is meeting the needs both of the press and of the university.

Multiple submissions. According to some press directors, multiple submissions are here. A promising manuscript is not likely to be rejected out of hand simply because the author states that it has been submitted to other publishers at the same time. Less than a decade ago multiple submissions were regarded as unprofessional or unethical. Today, the average press director may still prefer the traditional system whereby authors approach one press at a time or query several presses to ascertain interest in a manuscript before submitting it, in turn, to those responding affirmatively. This procedure is more orderly and economical of their time. But criticisms from authors impatient with delays have led directors to take a more tolerant view of multiple submissions *if they are openly made*. No doubt some presses will refuse to consider manuscripts submitted simultaneously elsewhere, and others may give low priority to multiple submissions at certain times. Thus, to say that the strong prejudice against multiple submissions has softened does not necessarily mean that authors in general will be better off than they were, though some are likely to be. Much will depend on how heavy the additional burden of manuscript reading becomes and on the discrimination of authors in selecting where to submit their manuscripts. Because of the much smaller numbers involved and the higher cost of preparing multiple copies of long manuscripts, the threat of inundation appears much less serious for book publishers than for journal editors.

We do not propose a recommendation on this issue because a period of testing is already under way, which may lead to a redefined standard of behavior that will recognize the reasonableness of the author's concerns as well as of the publisher's fears of undue burdens and disorder.

One requirement must be met by authors, however, if the process is to be accepted by most presses. Even press directors tolerant of multiple submissions insist that authors acknowledge that they have submitted the manuscript for consideration elsewhere. This gives the press the option of deciding whether to invest time in evaluating the manuscript.

ENLARGING THE MARKET

Nothing would serve the cause of scholarly publishing better than a substantial increase in the number of copies sold of every title. Larger printings would keep unit costs in check and perhaps lead to reductions in price, which might lead to even further increases in sales. Increased unit sales would generate more money for advertising, which, in turn, could lead to higher sales. Higher sales would yield greater royalties to authors, and rich authors might be persuaded to buy more books. And so on. As an alternative to the familiar and dispiriting trend of rising prices and falling sales, the possibilities of this scenario are pleasant to contemplate. There have been periods when scholarly book sales have been locked into an upward spiral. Why not again?

In the long run the possibility cannot be ruled out, but there are no grounds for optimism for the near future in the face of demographic trends, college enrollment trends, and economic forecasts. Regardless of what authors and publishers do, trends in book publishing cannot escape the influence of broad economic and social change.

To some extent the problem of how to expand the sale of books reflects the limitations of the distribution system. Most' scholarly books are not available in bookstores, even on college campuses, and not all bookstores are willing to place orders for single copies. Thus, as our survey showed, scholars have become accustomed to writing directly to publishers for what they want. They generally are satisfied with the service, or resigned to it, but the old refrain that it ought to be easier to place an order for a book continues to be heard. Are alternative arrangements feasible? For example, it has been asked, could libraries help in the process by taking orders, so that a reader who saw in a library a book worth owning could order a copy for personal use by filling out a form available on the spot? Authors are always certain—and scholars in general seem to be fairly confident—that if books were more readily available, they would be purchased in greater quantities. Only a small fraction of the 40,000 or more books published in a year show up in bookstores, and unless they are classics or are required for classroom use from semester to semester, they are unlikely to be kept in stock very long. If bookstores cannot manage the job, can libraries help? The suggestion awaits testing, and the fact remains that the rich diversity of book publishing is to some extent self-defeating.

We have no innovation in distribution to suggest that will miraculously help reverse the downward trend in average sales per title. To call for a drastic reduction in the number of titles published might improve the picture statistically only to set back the cause of scholarly communication in the process. The way to increase sales is to do everything a little better—from the writing of books, to the promotion, warehousing and shipping of them. In particular we favor an increase in the proportion of titles published simultaneously in hardbound and paperback editions and an expansion in the effort of presses to sell more books abroad.

PAPERBACKS AND DUAL EDITIONS.   The dwindling sale of hardbound books, reflecting the decline in library sales and the resistance of individual buyers to rising prices, has stimulated interest in the publication of a greater number of scholarly titles simultaneously in hardbound and paperback editions. Some publishers believe that such dual editions can play an important role in increasing the dissemination of scholarly knowledge, which is their principal mission, and in reducing their deficits, which constitute the principal threat to their survival.

American university presses publish one new title in seven in simultaneous cloth and paper editions and nearly the same number in paper editions only (see table 3.6). They continue to publish two out of three titles in cloth editions alone.

Table 3.6. Classification of Editions Published by Members of the AAUP, 1977

Edition	American presses (64)	Other presses (10)	All presses (74)
New titles	2,255	1,396	3,651
Cloth only	1,654	} 1,294	} 3,239
Paper only	291		
Paper and cloth	310	102	412
Revised editions	83	20	103
Cloth only	36	6	42
Paper only	33	5	38
Cloth and paper	14	9	23
Paper editions of earlier cloth titles	209	36	245
Total titles	2,547	1,452	3,999

Source: Association of American University Presses.

Practices vary widely. For example, among large presses (defined here as those issuing seventy-five titles a year in new or revised editions), Princeton publishes more than one new title in five in dual editions, whereas California publishes fewer than one in ten and M.I.T. one in twenty. California, Chicago, M.I.T., and Yale, among the large presses, put a heavier reliance on the publication of paperback editions of previously published hardbound titles. By postponing the paperback for a year or two after the publication of the original edition, they are better able to assess the demand for the paperback, and they also are protected against erosion of the sales of the cloth edition that generally takes place when a paperback is issued simultaneously.

Among medium-sized presses (those publishing twenty to seventy-five titles a year), Nebraska publishes a third of its titles in dual editions, whereas some presses in this class publish only an occasional title in both editions or none at all. A number of small presses (fewer than twenty titles a year) publish no simultaneous cloth and paper editions.

Over the decade ending in 1971, tabulations by the AAUP show little change in the proportion of titles being published in dual editions by presses as a group, but substantial changes in the practices of some presses.

Simultaneous publication of paper and cloth editions achieves three objectives. First, the availability of the paperback brings the book within reach of more individual scholars. Second, simultaneous publication means that the paperback is available a year or more earlier than it would be if the decision were postponed until after the market had been tested by the cloth edition. This gain in time is not important for many books in the humanities, but it is of considerable importance in the social sciences and sciences. Generally, whenever material is likely to become outdated in a few years, a paperback edition, if it is warranted, should be published simultaneously with the cloth edition. Third, it achieves some promotional efficiency because it eliminates the need for a separate effort to announce the paperback, and reduces the likelihood that those who hear of the cloth edition never learn of the paperback, or hear of it only after the lag of another couple of years.

The dual edition, on the other hand, exposes the publisher to risks. First, sales of the paperback may cut into the sales of the hardbound edition by more than expected, with the result that revenues may fall far below the target used in establishing the print run and price. Second, sales of the paperback may be lower than estimated, with the result that total sales of the book are not much greater than they would have been with a cloth edition only. If so, total revenues may fall 10, 20, or 50 percent below what was necessary to break even. In these circumstances, what is the appropriate strategy for the university press?

We believe first that a change in attitude is required. It has been all too common for publishers to assume that books will be published in cloth editions alone.

The library is the basic market for most scholarly books. Libraries prefer durable bindings, and so the tendency has been to estimate sales on the basis of a cloth edition. Publication of a simultaneous paperback edition is considered only when its use in college courses appears to be highly likely. This is a safe approach and not an unreasonable policy from a financial point of view. But scholarly publishers have an obligation to go beyond the safe approach. We think that the dual edition ought to be explored, not as an exception, but routinely in the publication plan for a high proportion of books.

Not every book. The market for some books is inevitably small. Those who need highly specialized works—primarily research libraries—will buy irrespective of the prices (assuming that they bear some reasonable relation to the prices of comparable books), and virtually no additional buyers will purchase them if the prices are only half as great as prices of the cloth edition or a third as great.

For another class of books—those that are very expensive—the price of the paperback would have to be ridiculously high in order not to erode the market for the expensive edition. For such books, if they turn out to be exceptionally well received, a separate paperback edition might well be issued some years later, if the contents are of lasting interest or usefulness.

But for most books, university publishers should at least consider the paperback potential by preparing alternative estimates comparing (1) costs, probable sales, and price for a clothbound edition only; and (2) costs, probable sales, and prices for a dual edition under different assumptions. One assumption is the expectation that a book will be used as supplementary reading in courses. If these are advanced courses, the size of the orders might be small—say, 10 to 30 copies—but still the printing of a paperback edition of at least 2,000 to 3,000 copies would be warranted. This kind of estimate is frequently made, though not as routinely as it might be.

The second assumption—and the one commonly overlooked—is the possibility that a paperback edition will attract a large number of individual buyers. A first-rate book with some breadth of appeal, which might be printed in a cloth edition of 2,000 copies at $17.50, might warrant a printing of 3,000 copies in a dual edition—1,400 cloth and 1,600 paper—if the paperback were priced, say, at $7.95. The decision to print a dual edition would be justified if the additional sales income from the paperback more than offset (1) loss of revenue resulting from the decline in clothbound sales, and (2) the increase in costs resulting from the production of the paperback —that is, manufacturing costs plus other costs such as the cost of managing two separate inventories. Sometimes it may be necessary to increase the price of the clothbound edition slightly in order to make a dual edition feasible. The advantage to individual buyers is thus partly offset by the slight additional burden on some libraries. But since a dual edition reduces costs for other libraries that buy the paperback edition for extra copies needed for reserve room use, the overall effect on libraries as a group may well be neutral. It is even possible that libraries may benefit from lower prices. If the paperback market is sufficiently large, it may permit a lower price for a hardbound book issued as part of a dual edition than would have been feasible if only a cloth edition were published.

In a number of instances it has been shown that a dual edition will expand total sales by about 50 percent or more despite a reduction of perhaps 15 to 20 percent in the sale of clothbound copies. In these circumstances presses will be better off financially with a dual edition than with a cloth edition alone. More important, a greater number of copies will be sold, and as one university publisher put it, "This is a kind of 'profit' in scholarly publishing."

The stress on dual editions whenever feasible is a minority view among university press publishers. But it has worked for some presses, and we believe it can work for many more. What particularly recommends it at this juncture in the history of scholarly publishing is that if library purchases continue to decline or merely level off, publishers are going to be hard pressed to keep book prices within reach of individuals unless they can expand single-copy sales to scholars. The importance scholars attach to their private libraries suggests that this market can be enlarged.

What we recommend here is not that presses seek to publish some arbitrary number of books in paper and cloth editions, but that they begin to explore the dual edition alternative as a matter of course. If, instead of one in seven, the number of books published simultaneously in two editions were one in five, or one in four, the contribution to the dissemination of scholarly information would be substantial.

This hypothetical discussion has not come to grips with the crucial question. How does a publisher know whether it is possible to sell an additional 1,000 copies of a book by issuing a paperback edition? The answer depends ultimately on experience. Marketing managers can devise ways to compare a new book with other similar ones in the past, in the light of current conditions. But books are sufficiently different from each other to introduce an element of uncertainty into each publishing decision—and it is here that the art of publishing comes into play. Some publishers will make the right decision most of the time, some will not, and some probably will continue not to try.

Many publishers will not find this point of view persuasive. They will prefer to test the market with a clothbound edition before issuing a paperback. They can surely argue that if the paperback is issued a year or two later, no great loss will have been suffered with respect to most books in the humanities. But that is not the whole story. We doubt that many presses will go back to press merely to issue 1,000 copies of a paperback. The cost of doing so would be substantially higher than the costs would have been for a paperback put out as part of a dual edition. Thus, we believe far fewer books will appear in paperback if the publisher follows the more conservative course of testing the market first.

From the standpoint of a press director, nonetheless, the error of not maximizing copies sold does not show up in the balance sheet, and thus it is easy to live with. The write-off of unsold inventory does show up, however. Thus, there is a greater incentive for prudence than for boldness, at least until the number of copies sold is given greater weight in assessing the perform- ance of a press. To offset the understandable reluctance of press directors to assume additional risks, foundations should consider offering subsidies to encourage dual editions.

Recommendation 3.7.   Paperback editions
More scholarly titles should be published simultaneously in cloth and paperback editions as a step toward widening the dissemination of scholarly research.

FOREIGN SALES.   A major market for American scholarly books exists abroad. In a study for the Enquiry, Datus C. Smith, Jr., comes to the surprising conclusion that the sales of university press books in foreign countries could be doubled by effective promotion, simplification of market- ing procedures, and other steps that presses can make themselves.[19] This estimate seems overly optimistic, but there is at least widespread support for the view that the foreign market has not yet been effectively developed. The potential for enlarging the market is greater for technical and scientific works than for studies in the humanities, but the humanities also stand to benefit from higher sales and perhaps indirectly from the improved position of a press resulting from the increased sales of scientific titles.

Smith's estimate is based on his analysis of comments by a group of 328 men and women who were either interviewed personally or who responded to requests for facts and opinions. More than half the group, including book importers in fifty-nine countries, were from outside the United States.

19. Datus C. Smith, Jr., "Foreign Distribution of American University Press Books," a report to the National Enquiry, June 30, 1977, p. 5. The discussion of foreign distribution is adapted from Smith's report.

University presses as a group obtained about 15 percent of their sales volume in 1975 from sales abroad, which is substantially higher than the proportion of foreign sales by American publishers generally. The percentage of sales made to foreign buyers varies widely among presses, even among those of comparable size. The fields in which they publish, the relative emphasis on regional material, and the effort they put into developing the foreign market all play a role. Nearly half the foreign volume for presses as a group comes from the United Kingdom and Western Europe and only 1.6 percent from Latin America. Variations in sales by country can be accounted for largely by differences in education, in the percentage of the population with a reading knowledge of English, and in affluence. Difficulties in the exchange of currencies also play a role.

Foreign buyers cite a number of obstacles to the purchase of American books. Some of them—such as the proliferation of titles in recent years, the trend toward increasing specialization, and the narrowness of the American point of view—are beyond the control of individual presses. Nor can presses do anything about censorship in foreign countries, poor delivery systems, and the shortage of foreign exchange. But presses are not helpless to deal with criticisms leveled at their slowness in answering requests for information, in shipping books, and in rectifying errors. Equally troubling to foreign buyers is the lack of uniformity in the procedures used by different presses for handling foreign orders. The practice of adding a surcharge to the price of foreign orders to recover the additional costs of doing business abroad, has been criticized by foreign buyers. Many presses consider it to be necessary, however, because additional costs of selling books abroad are high and must be covered.

Other shortcomings brought to light in the Enquiry study relate to book promotion and distribution for the foreign market. Very little promotional material is sent directly to scholars; most of it is directed to libraries. Outside of the United Kingdom, Western Europe, and Canada, there is inadequate representation of university publishers and little warehousing of stock. As a result, shipments are slow to reach their destinations, and books that are ordered out of a misunderstanding of their contents or are otherwise unsatisfactory can seldom be returned.

Steps to reduce these complaints are within reach of the presses acting collectively if not individually. There is a great need for subject matter circulars and catalogs, seasonal announcements, general catalogs, exhibits, review copies, and a possible revival of something like *Scholarly Books in*

America, which apparently had a substantial following abroad during the years in which it was produced.

Opportunities to build rapport between university presses and the book world abroad also need to be actively pursued. Ideally, the names of scholars who have visited the United States should be placed on mailing lists so that established relationships will not be lost. But there is no existing mechanism to assure that this will be done. Presses might also make greater use of the International Book Information Service (IBIS), which lists 350,000 individual scholars and more than 40,000 libraries outside the United States, only one-fourth of whom are in the British Isles. Lists can be selected by geographic area and subject matter for the promotion of American books. Although the cost of using the IBIS list is considered high, it might not be out of line for joint promotional efforts by several presses.

Foreign booksellers and librarians, dizzied by the variety of systems of order taking, back-ordering, billing, shipping, and paying, are especially interested in the standardization of sales procedures. Similarly strong are their pleas for increased stocking of U.S. books abroad.

Over and above these specifics, presses need to increase their personal representation abroad. Jobbers perform an essential service as order takers, bill collectors, and factors who make it possible for presses to get paid promptly for their shipments. But they are unable to provide the kind of promotional service that is required.

Finally, presses need to keep flexible in their dealings with foreign buyers, recognizing the range of obstacles to the flow of books across international borders and accepting direct orders, orders placed through export jobbing firms, or payment through UNESCO coupons—depending on the circumstances of the buyers—rather than insisting on a single mode of payment that is convenient for the presses.

If the presses can improve their performance, they will have a greater claim for assistance from government and foundations. One important form of government assistance would be the revival of the Informational Media Guaranty Program, which for several years made it possible for buyers in developing countries to pay for books from commercial as well as nonprofit publishers in local currency, without having to secure dollar-exchange for the purpose.

A major role could also be played by the International Communications Agency (ICA), successor to the U.S. Information Agency (USIA). The ICA could assist in the international communication of scholarly work by distributing promotional material for scholarly books and by strengthening its program of book exhibits and presentations of significant publications to scholars and officials abroad.

Much of the effort to improve foreign sales will require an increase in activities undertaken jointly by university presses. Some may require "up-front" money from foundations to finance the initial stages of joint warehousing, promotional distributions, and so on. The need for press, government, and foundation cooperation in this area is great indeed.

Recommendation 3.8. The market for books abroad
We recommend a vigorous effort to promote sales of scholarly books abroad through (a) collaboration and improvements in service that can be undertaken by the presses themselves; (b) the reestablishment of a government guarantee program that would make it easier to surmount currency exchange problems, import restrictions, and other impediments to international trade; and (c) foundation support to help finance the start-up costs of new ventures.

OUTSIDE SOURCES OF SUPPORT
Since scholarly presses were established to publish manuscripts that were not commercially attractive, they have always been subsidized. Some subsidies have been indirect, such as the provision of free office space. Others have been direct, such as subsidies for publication of individual titles, general support grants from foundations or private individuals, and support from parent universities that have been willing to make up deficits.

THE ROLE OF UNIVERSITIES WITHOUT PRESSES. The traditional system of *ad hoc* subsidization has worked fairly well in the United States, but it has not been equitable. It has put most of the burden for scholarly publishing on some sixty universities that have established presses. The other 1,500 or so universities and four-year colleges have been able to enjoy a free ride, unless they established programs to subsidize publications of work by scholars on their campuses, as some have done. Thus, we think that the future participation of universities without presses in the process of scholarly communication merits closer scrutiny, along with an examination of the role of foundations.[20]

20. For a press director's view of this question, see John Ervin, Jr., "When a University Has No Press," *Scholarly Publishing* (October 1976).

There are a number of ways in which universities without presses can help, ranging from title subsidies to participation in a consortium, such as the University Press of New England.

The broadest program would be one in which 100 or 200 universities offered title subsidies annually (or every other year) of $1,000 to $3,000 each to support the publication of meritorious manuscripts produced on campus—manuscripts that otherwise would probably not be published without a subsidy, either because the work would be unusually costly to print or would be of interest to only a very small audience. The published manuscript would recognize the role of the sponsoring university with a note on the title page stating "Published in cooperation with the ———— College by the ———— University Press." Smaller colleges and universities could participate in such a program on an *ad hoc* basis with smaller grants. A cooperative effort to encourage widespread participation might well be considered by a scholarly organization, such as the American Council of Learned Societies, which is especially concerned about sustaining the publication of works in the humanities. Foundation support in the form of a matching grant would be useful in encouraging universities to participate.

A university that seeks a more active role may consider establishing a series of books under its own imprint—either for a special area such as the humanities or for any manuscripts produced on its campus. The series would be published by an established press which would give appropriate recognition to the sponsoring institution. A subsidy for one or more titles a year would be sufficient to keep a series active.

A still more active role would be partnership in an established press. Small university presses should be encouraged to strengthen themselves by establishing consortia along the lines of the University Press of New England.

In short, there are several alternatives whereby universities can join in the communication of scholarly knowledge and help strengthen the financial underpinnings of scholarly publishing. These alternatives should have special appeal to those universities that have considered establishing presses but have backed away because of the cost. Subsidizing a series of books or individual titles would be far less costly and could gain recognition for the university while providing assistance to individual scholars.

Recommendation 3.9. The role of universities without presses

To broaden support for scholarly publishing, universities without presses should become active participants in the publishing process as sponsors of work produced on their campuses.

THE ROLE OF FOUNDATIONS.   A few foundations have long recognized the key role of university presses in the dissemination of scholarly materials. In 1956 and in 1962 the Ford Foundation made grants totaling $2,721,000 to a group of university presses "to stimulate scholarly publication in the humanities and social sciences."[21]

More recently, the Andrew W. Mellon Foundation made two substantial grants to subsidize the publication of the work of young scholars in the humanities and humanistic social sciences. The first of these, made in 1972 and totaling $2.1 million, went to twenty-four presses. In 1975 a second series of grants amounting to $1.4 million was made to twenty-five presses. At the time of each distribution, Mellon granted an additional $250,000 for subsidizing qualified manuscripts submitted by other university presses; these programs were administered by the American Council of Learned Societies.

While it is too early to judge the impact on scholarly publishing by the second series of Mellon grants, there is strong evidence that the funds made available in 1972 were useful for humanistic scholarship. Presses receiving the first Mellon grants maintained through 1976 a higher percentage of publications in the humanities than did other presses. Further, from 1973 through June 1977, a total of 253 titles were published with support from the 1972 grants. A large majority of these 253 titles were in the humanities, and, we estimate, represent upwards of 16 percent of all humanities titles published by university presses during this period. More significant, however, is that most of these 253 books were written by young scholars who were enabled to publish their first books during a period when publication had become increasingly competitive and difficult.

The Ford and Mellon grants, while large and dramatic, only illustrate the concern the foundations have had for scholarly communication over the years. The Rockefeller Foundation has a history of support dating back to 1924 when it gave $100,000 to each of two university presses—Chicago and North Carolina. It also contributed $250,000 to the support of the university press project, beginning in 1960, to publish works of Latin American scholarship.

Despite these notably successful experiences, the history of press–foundation relationships has been less than satisfactory in many respects, both for the foundations and presses. The foundations have often not been given enough information about the key role of publishing in the research

21. Datus Smith, Jr., "Foundations and Scholarly Publishing," a report to the National Enquiry. Much of the following discussion is abridged from Smith's report.

process and about the disciplines and subjects most in need of support. They have had no guidelines about how to proceed most effectively in the support of dissemination activities.

At the same time, the presses—and scholars—have encountered widespread indifference among many private foundations to publication problems. Even some of the nation's largest foundations have made it known that they will not support publication, despite their generosity in support of research. They have not yet been persuaded that the task of research is not completed until the results have been brought to the attention of those who can make use of them—which requires either publication or some other form of dissemination.

Similarly, the federal government's support of dissemination activities has been less than satisfactory. Large amounts of money have been made available by the National Science Foundation over the past thirty years. Little of this money, however, has gone to university presses, largely it may be assumed, because these presses publish sparingly in the natural sciences where funds have been most available. Grants for the dissemination of scholarly research funded by the National Science Foundation have gone primarily to nonprofit journals in the sciences where the use of page charges is common. Very little has gone to the support of scientific monographs.

The National Endowment for the Humanities followed an even more restricted policy. When it was created in 1965, largely through the efforts of humanists working with a small number of federal legislators, its charter included support of both research and its dissemination. During its early years, however, its small budget was devoted almost entirely to scholarly research and to staff support. As funding grew, the National Endowment extended its support of research, but refused to allocate funds to the dissemination of research. Efforts by the presses to document the need for funds to support publication of projects sponsored by the National Endowment met with no success.

Following the appointment in 1977 of a new chairman of the National Endowment and instructions from the Congress to carry out a program for funding publications, the policy was changed. We welcome the change and urge that publication subsidies be provided not only for research sponsored by the Endowment, but also for research that is funded by other sponsors or research that is carried out without any supporting grants. Much humanistic research and writing, for example, is conducted without special funding. In any event, both scholars and their publishers (university and commercial) stand to benefit in the near future from the new direction taken by the National Endowment.

The experience of presses indicates that neither private foundations nor government agencies fully appreciate that the creation and dissemination of scholarly knowledge is a single, integrated, continuous process. To make a grant of $50,000 or $100,000 which leads to the production of a significant work but to refuse to provide a much smaller sum to guarantee its publication and dissemination fails to recognize an essential link in the system of scholarly communication. It thereby reduces the effective functioning of that system.

We are not proposing that every major grant be accompanied by a supplemental award to guarantee publication. Neither publishers nor foundation executives who are sympathetic to subsidizing publishing think such assurance of publication is desirable. Respondents replying to our Survey of Scholars also think grants for research and for publication should be made separately. What we suggest is that foundations which make grants for research make known their willingness to consider supplementary grants for the publication of outstanding work. The decision to subsidize publication, however, should not be made until the research manuscript has been evaluated by a peer review process and judged to be worthy of publication. For example, acceptance by a scholarly press would provide grounds for an application for a publication grant.

If the inseparability of research and dissemination is recognized, foundations may want to consider better ways to link the two activities. One proposal is to establish a pool of qualified professional publishing consultants to advise private or governmental foundations. Since the economics and operating characteristics of publishing are not well known to scholars and foundation administrators, a publishing specialist can play an important role in assessing the need for a subsidy and the most effective way of providing it. The choice of publisher should be left to the author. Many different approaches can be developed to implement this suggestion, and each organization should be free to select one that reflects its own style and philosophy.

For many projects, of course, book publication may not be the most appropriate form of dissemination. If the audience is small or if timeliness is of great importance, a conference or workshop may be more appropriate, supplemented by distribution of offset copies of a summary paper. Or because of the brevity of a report, journal publication may be more appropriate, with a subsidy provided for distribution of offprints. The nature of the audience and of the subject matter should determine the form of dissemination.

The foregoing discussion is not intended to suggest that the role of foundations in subsidizing publication should be limited to the support of research that they have funded. It is intended rather to suggest that this is an important and neglected area that merits attention. There will be a continuing need to subsidize other meritorious work, and, more important, foundation funding will be needed to finance organizational and technological improvements in the system. These include marketing experiments such as the establishment of cooperative warehousing and shipping facilities in the United States or abroad, and the establishment of a committee to promote further discussion of the nature and direction of technological change.

Recommendation 3.10.   A broader role for foundations
We recommend greater support for scholarly communication—grants for systemwide improvements, funds to encourage collaboration among publishers, and title subsidies (particularly for the publication of foundation-supported research that has been judged to be meritorious).

CONCLUSION

University presses have largely recovered from the financial difficulties of the mid-1970s, and they enjoy the respect of authors, readers, and university administrators. Nevertheless, their future is far from assured. Between the most successful and the least, the gap in performance and resources is large enough to cause concern for those that require the greatest subsidies. Furthermore, all presses are caught in the squeeze between rising costs and the resistance of buyers to rising prices. The upward pressure on publishing costs also increases the difficulty of deciding what to publish and how many copies to print. These and other problems that emerged during the 1970s, such as the increasing competition for a share of the library acquisitions budget, are not likely to disappear in the near future.

Presses are not without recourse, however. Collaborative efforts in book publishing, as in journal publishing, clearly can improve efficiency. By concentrating their efforts on editorial initiatives and marketing strategy—while shifting the burden of warehousing, data processing and related functions to a stronger press or to a consortium—small presses can maintain a vital role for themselves. Large presses will need to experiment with ways to reduce the downward trend in the unit sales of new titles through expansion of paperback editions and enlargement of the foreign market.

At its best, however, scholarly publishing is not a self-supporting endeavor. It should not be expected to fully pay its way. Help must be provided not only by universities that have presses but from other universities as well, since they, too, have a stake in the quality of scholarly communications and in the research of scholars on their campuses. Those foundations that have generously supported scholarly presses in the past will be called on again, and so will scores of other foundations that have not supported publication in the past. In the diversity of scholarly work, there is ample opportunity for donors to choose the kind of publication that they prefer to support. Government funds will be needed, too. In short, collaboration among publishers and the extension of the system to include institutions and donors that have not previously contributed are key elements in the long-run planning of scholarly publishers.

CHAPTER 4

Research Libraries and Scholarly Communication

The nation's research libraries are clearly central to the system of scholarly communication, but a few introductory remarks are necessary to place this chapter in the broader context of the Enquiry's concerns. The analysis is concentrated on the nation's research libraries, largely affiliated with major universities, rather than on the entire library system. Since these libraries must serve all disciplines within the university, the discussion necessarily ranges beyond the humanities. Furthermore, the focus is not on libraries as self-contained entities, but rather on their role in fostering scholarship and in aiding the transfer of knowledge from mind to mind and generation to generation. Consequently, no attempt is made to discuss all aspects of library operation and finance, important as these topics may be; instead, only those aspects of finance and management that bear on the ability of libraries to meet the needs of research and scholarship are examined. The interrelationships of libraries, presses, journals, and scholars define and limit our interests and determine the approach taken toward libraries. We believe that this perspective is consistent with the purposes and objectives of the nation's research libraries, and that our recommendations may help the institutions to realize those objectives. In no sense, however, can this chapter be viewed as a comprehensive treatment of the many difficult issues facing research libraries that transcend the concerns of the Enquiry.

Three of the Enquiry's commissioned studies did bear on libraries, either as part of a larger investigation or as a focused examination of a topic of explicit interest to the project. First, several questions about libraries were included in the Survey of Scholars conducted by the Enquiry: the scholar as author, and the scholar as reader.[1] Second, the Enquiry joined with the

[1] Janet D. Griffith, "The Survey of Scholars: Relationships between the Scholars and Other Estates" (Research Triangle Park, N.C., Research Triangle Institute, February 1978; processed).

National Science Foundation in supporting Bernard Fry and Herbert White in a follow-up study of their 1975 report on library acquisition policies.[2] The earlier Fry–White report had drawn attention to the striking shift that had occurred during the early 1970s in the proportion of library budgets being spent on journals at the expense of books, and their 1978 report updated the earlier statistics with three more years of information.[3] Third, with support from the Enquiry and the National Endowment for the Humanities, Hugh Cline and Loraine Sinnott conducted detailed field investigation of the decision-making process surrounding collection development in seven academic libraries,[4] a case-study approach that complemented the more aggregate data collection of Fry and White. Our discussion of research libraries and scholarly communication begins with a summary of the pertinent findings of these commissioned studies.

THE SURVEY OF SCHOLARS

For this survey, discussed in some of its aspects in chapters 2 and 3, a sample of scholars was drawn,[5] representing seven disciplines in the humanities and social sciences: anthropology, classics, English, history, philosophy, Romance languages, and sociology.[6] Information pertaining to libraries was collected through nine specific questions on library usage and through several broader questions focused on the way scholars acquire and use books, journals, and other materials of scholarship.

In interpreting the survey responses, it is useful to distinguish between the library's role as a repository for documents, monographs, journals, and the other raw materials of scholarship, and its role as a mediator and facilitator of scholarly research through reference services and other assistance. Insofar as their personal needs as scholars are concerned, the survey

---

[2] Bernard M. Fry and Herbert S. White, "Economics and Interaction of the Publisher-Library Relationship in the Production and Use of Scholarly and Research Journals" (Washington, D.C., National Science Foundation, November 1975; processed).

[3] Bernard M. Fry and Herbert S. White, "Impact of Economic Pressures on American Libraries and Their Decisions Concerning Scholarly and Research Journal Acquisition and Retention" (Washington, D.C., National Science Foundation, June 1978; processed).

[4] Hugh F. Cline and Loraine T. Sinnott, "Organizational Case Studies of Collection Development Policies and Practices" (Educational Testing Service, February 1979; processed).

[5] The following summary is adapted from Griffith, "The Survey of Scholars," pp. 41–45.

[6] See chap. 2 of this volume, footnote 8, for additional details of the Survey's scope and coverage.

evidence strongly suggests that the respondents are mainly interested in the library as a repository, and that they have somewhat less interest in the library's other services to scholarship. This finding is consistent with responses to the questions about the most severe problems they see in the communication system. After high book prices, the most frequently mentioned problem is inadequate collections of books in their institution's library.

The respondents report making heavy use of library collections. Two-thirds borrow more than twenty books from the library in a year, and one-third borrow more than fifty. It should be noted in this context that two-thirds describe their personal library as adequate or excellent for their research needs, and thus use the library to supplement their own collections, with borrowing concentrated on costly, specialized, or less frequently used volumes. On the other hand, there is evidence that scholars encounter problems in making use of the library as a source of needed volumes; 83 percent report that in a typical month they find that at least one book they need is not listed in the card catalog; and 84 percent find one or more books a month unavailable because the books are either in use or are lost.

Roughly as many respondents acquired the last book they read by purchase as those who acquired it through the library. And the library plays only a minor role in the process of learning about new books in their field; only 4 percent learned of the book they most recently purchased by browsing in the library, and two-thirds made no effort even to check whether the library had a copy before they placed their order. Interlibrary loan was also negligible as a source of the most recently read book.

Few scholars report the lack of bibliographic and reference works as an important failing in the system of scholarly communication. This lack of concern with the quality and availability of reference services appears to reflect an absence of need for such services (or a belief that services to meet their particular needs could not be provided) as much as satisfaction with available reference works and services.

These broad generalizations must be qualified by differences that appear when responses are analyzed by institutional affiliation, academic rank, and scholarly discipline. The advantage of major universities in library collections is evident from the responses to a question about the most severe problems in the communication system. For scholars in these universities, library book collections do not even rank among the six most frequently mentioned problems, while for those in less-developed universities and in colleges, inadequate book collections rank second among the problems mentioned (behind book prices, which is first for all groups). Although library journal collections are less frequently identified as a problem, they rank among the most often mentioned problems for the less-developed universities and for the colleges.

Junior scholars are relatively heavy users of the library. More assistant than associate or full professors report making five or more lengthy searches in an average year; and more report that they have borrowed a larger number of books in recent years. Among the problems mentioned by scholars, inadequate library book collections are mentioned somewhat more by assistant and associate professors than by full professors, and the two lower ranks mentioned library journal collections as among the top six problems, while full professors did not. The full professors' greater satisfaction with library collections may reflect the fact that many of them have helped shape the institution's collection to their research needs. With tighter library budgets, younger faculty may be able to do this less in the future than the senior faculty did in the past.

Junior faculty also reported greater needs for—or interest in— improved mechanisms of access to scholarly literature. Fewer assistant professors than other ranks think that most articles and books important to their teaching and research are brought to their attention in a reasonable amount of time (60 percent, compared with 79 percent of full professors), and more think that computer-based bibliographic searches would be useful for research in their field (67 percent of assistant professors say they would be useful, compared with 53 percent of full professors). Thus, while library collections dominate the concerns of scholars at all ranks, junior scholars show a particular interest in reference services.

Two differences among humanistic disciplines that are important for scholars' relationships to the libraries are the differing emphases placed on monographs and journals, and the degree to which personal libraries meet the needs of scholarship. Historians—despite the relatively large size of their own libraries—find personal libraries less adequate for their needs than do other scholars. They use the institution's library heavily (and report increasing use in recent years), and rank the library's book collection second among their problems, after book prices. Historians are also increasingly heavy users of journals, and rank inadequate library journal collections among the major communication problems they face as scholars. Philosophers, by contrast, have relatively large personal libraries and express considerable satisfaction with them; their use of the library is low relative to the other disciplines (both in number of searches made and number of volumes borrowed). These differences are reflected in the fact that philosophers alone did not rank inadequate library book collections among the top problems they face. For the other disciplines, library book collections are among the most frequently mentioned problems.

In summary, the survey supports the following conclusions about scholars' perceptions of their relationship to the library. First, inadequate library collections, particularly monographic collections, are a major concern to scholars in the humanities; as book prices have risen, scholars report a net reduction in their purchases of books, combined with some compensating increase in library use. While favorably disposed toward interlibrary loan, the scholars did not report making extensive use of it. Second, future problems may be particularly acute in the less-developed universities and colleges, especially if expectations of scholarly productivity increase in these institutions. Although responses of faculty members at all ranks and institutions indicate considerable bibliographic independence, junior scholars report somewhat more concern with the effectiveness of information sources in bringing works to their attention promptly, and have somewhat greater interest than do senior scholars in computer-assisted bibliographic services. With a continued increase in the amount of scholarly materials, demand for such services may increase. And, finally, differences among humanistic disciplines in their needs and style of scholarship need to be taken into account in planning subsequent library development.

The scholars' stress on development of their local collection and their relative lack of interest in bibliographic services run counter to the directions in library development advocated in this report and supported by most careful students of the subject. The sheer growth of written and recorded materials coupled with inevitable limitations on library budgets suggests that the understandable desire of scholars for local self-sufficiency in library resources will increasingly fall short of attainment. Adjustments in scholarly habits and attitudes toward library usage will clearly be required in coming years, and the education of faculty and students in new library techniques and services must be included among the librarians' most important responsibilities.

THE FRY–WHITE SURVEY

In 1975 Bernard Fry and Herbert White, members of the Graduate Library School at Indiana University, submitted a report to the National

Science Foundation on library–publisher relationships, and subsequently published their findings in a book entitled *Publishers and Libraries: A Study of Scholarly and Research Journals.*[7] Based on a survey covering 400 libraries and 250 journals over the period 1969–73, the study reported on economic conditions, budgetary pressures, behavioral and decision-making patterns, as well as on attitudes and perceptions of librarians and publishers. Among their most striking findings was a pronounced shift over the four years in library allocations from the book to the serials budget. In large academic libraries, for example, the ratio of monograph to serials expenditures dropped from 2:1 in 1969 to 1.16:1 in 1973. The significance of this trend for scholarly book publishing—if it continued—was clear and ominous, for scholarly presses depend heavily on library sales. Consequently, updating the Fry–White study was a high priority, and the Enquiry joined with the National Science Foundation in supporting that effort. Their second report was submitted in June 1978, with major findings of interest to the Enquiry summarized here.[8]

1. LIBRARY BUDGET INCREASES FOR 1973–76. Academic libraries did not, during the budget period 1973–76, fare as well as the institutions in which they are housed. In state-supported academic institutions, the library budget rose by 9.5 percent a year, while the college or university budget increased by 10.4 percent a year. Large state-supported academic libraries in particular fared worse than the institution as a whole, increasing their budgets at an annual 8.6 percent, while the institution's budget rose 9.9 percent.

2. TRANSFER OF FUNDS FROM THE MATERIALS TO THE SALARY BUDGET. Findings of the earlier (1969–73) study indicated a steady shift (at the rate of about ½ percent a year) from the materials to the salary budget in academic and public libraries. While the early data for 1973–76 indicated a continuation of this trend, it may have ceased in about 1974. Statistics for 1975 and 1976, while of insufficient length to constitute a trend, nevertheless point to an absence of budgetary transfers between the labor and materials budgets. This may be because budget categories are now separately allocated, without an opportunity to shift funds.

[7] Bernard M. Fry and Herbert S. White, *Publishers and Libraries: A Study of Scholarly and Research Journals* (Lexington, Mass., D.C. Heath, 1976).

[8] The following summary is adapted from Fry and White, "Impact of Economic Pressures," pp. 10–15.

3. ALLOCATION OF FUNDS TO THE MATERIALS BUDGET. Despite the apparent halt in budgetary shifts from the materials to the salary budget, the materials budget continues to receive a declining percentage of total funds allocated within the academic library. Growing percentages of the library budget are going to supplies and related materials, reflecting in part rapid price increases in these categories, and also some budgetary shifts, under which purchased data-base access and document-delivery services are playing a more prominent role.

4. ABILITY TO MAINTAIN THE LIBRARY COLLECTION. Although estimates of the growth of published material vary, even conservative approximations lead to the conclusion that few libraries are keeping up with the expansion of publication in their own fields of interests, and that most are in fact falling behind. This is particularly true for monographic purchases in academic libraries, which continue to decline.

5. BUDGETARY SHIFTS FROM THE BOOK TO THE SERIALS BUDGET. One of the most significant findings of the 1969–73 study was the dramatic shift in materials allocation from the book to the serials budget. Based on this rapid change, which endangers the validity of any monographic acquisitions program, the earlier study surmised that this rapid shift would have to decelerate or stop entirely. Data for 1973–76, however, clearly indicate that the shift of funds from the book to the serials budget continued unchecked in all types of libraries. Large academic libraries were, by 1976, spending 83 cents on books for every dollar spent on serials. Some libraries report an even more dramatic ratio. Interview responses indicate that these shifts reflect the priorities of the faculty to a greater extent than of the library staff, particularly in the physical and social sciences. Many faculty feel that serials must be renewed at all costs, to maintain continuity and currency. Monographic acquisitions represent, to many faculty, especially in these disciplines, a less urgent priority.

6. SHIFTS WITHIN THE PERIODICALS BUDGET. Despite the attempts to maintain as much of the serials budget as possible, academic libraries continued to face the need to reduce periodicals subscriptions. From the 1969–73 survey, the most prevalent tactics reported were decisions not to place new subscriptions and the cancellation of duplicates. Both these tactics continue to be heavily employed from 1973–76 reports, but for the first time a heavy incidence of cancellation of single and unique titles is reported.

7. MANAGEMENT DECISIONS. Although, as reported above, libraries began extensively, during 1973–76, to cancel unique subscriptions, the

survey failed to uncover any evidence that this largely resulted from consortia or network activities, or the perceived availability of the cancelled title on interlibrary loan. Decisions appear to be based on an evaluation of the specific title, or on a relative ranking of related titles, but only within the context of the collection, or of departmental priorities. Questions designed to determine who recommends, influences, or makes cancellation or placement decisions produced responses which indicate a complex interaction of librarians and faculty members, with heavy reliance, at least for recommended actions, on faculty members branch librarians, and subject specialists; and with little, if any, indication that local or regional holdings are taken into account.

8. INTERLIBRARY LOAN. Responding libraries reported a sharp increase in both interlibrary borrowing and lending. This may reflect the fact that, as materials acquisitions budgets fail to keep pace with cost increases and publication growth, individual libraries fall further behind and become more dependent on other library holdings. At the same time, however, libraries also report that availability on interlibrary loan does not affect their own acquisitions decisions. In short, it may be concluded that libraries borrow what they do not have, but that they do not cancel because they are able to borrow; they assume that nothing is too esoteric to be unavailable on loan.

9. PARTICIPATION IN CONSORTIA AND NETWORKS. Membership in consortia and networks is a continually growing phenomenon. More than 90 percent of large academic libraries belong to some sort of formal interlibrary organization, and these joiners belong to an average of almost three each. While membership in consortia and networks may be the required forerunner to cooperative activity in technical processing, acquisitions, and resource sharing, the survey revealed, at least at this stage, very little indication that library-management policies were closely affected by cooperative membership. Growing reliance on other libraries appears to come as a necessity as a library's own programs fail to keep pace with its needs, but there is little evidence of policy coordination and planning.

10. INCIDENCE OF COST-REDUCTION ACTIVITIES. Virtually all libraries report some cost-reduction activity, but it is surprising, in view of the evident financial constraints, that there is not a greater variety or range of such activities. Only about half the libraries in the survey report more than one tactic, and only about one-third report more than two. Cooperative cataloging arrangements far outdistance any other arrangements mentioned.

Reliance on purchased services in lieu of using their own manpower is not a frequently mentioned activity, which probably indicates that most libraries do not have total flexibility in transferring funds from one budget category to another. Nor is automation reported often as a major cost-reduction tactic.

11. INVOLVEMENT IN PERIODICALS MANAGEMENT DECISIONS. Responses indicate a wide variety of such involvements in academic libraries, particularly in recommendation for either acquisition or cancellation. Reference librarians, branch librarians, subject specialists, the library director, collection-development officers (where the posts exist), and committees all are reported as playing a role in the decision process. The role of the faculty is generally defined as being one of recommendation. Academic librarians on the project's Advisory Board, however, felt that responses to the questionnaire reflected some subjectivity and perhaps wishful thinking, and that the role of the faculty in the actual decision-making process is much greater.

The continued shift in library acquisition budgets from books to serials, noted in the second Fry–White report, was confirmed by the research of Fritz Machlup and his associates.[9] Table 4.1, taken from their study, reports the expenditures for books, serials, and other materials in 119 academic libraries over the seven years, 1970–76. The authors comment on the data as follows:

Table 4.1 reveals a highly important development of the 1970–1976 period: the crowding-out of book purchases by the expansion and inflation of the budget for serials. The relative share of library expenditures for books fell year after year, from 63.1 percent of total purchases of materials in 1970 to 47.3 percent in 1976. The share of serials purchases, on the other hand, increased from 32.0 percent in 1970 to 46.3 percent. These drastic budget shifts were associated with the very different rates of increases in purchases over the period. Total purchases increased by 39.1 percent: purchases of serials, however, increased by 101.1 percent, purchases of "other materials" by 80.4 percent, and purchases of books by only 4.3 percent.[10]

The findings of the Fry–White and Machlup surveys are consistent with the report from the scholars' survey that, next to the high price of books, inadequate library collections of monographs are the most severe problem

[9] Fritz Machlup, Kenneth W. Leeson, and associates, "Information Through the Printed Word: The Dissemination of Scholarly, Scientific, and Intellectual Knowledge" (New York, New York University, March 1978; processed).

[10] Ibid., pp. 6, 5, and 7.

Table 4.1. Expenditures for Books, Periodicals, and Other Materials, by 119 Libraries, 1970–76

Year	Total purchases	Books	Percentage of total	Serials	Percentage of total	Other materials	Percentage of total
1970	$44,419,000	$28,007,000	63.1	$14,236,000	32.0	$2,176,000	4.9
1971	44,571,000	26,338,000	59.1	15,797,000	35.4	2,435,000	5.5
1972	45,393,000	25,669,000	56.6	17,434,000	38.4	2,290,000	5.0
1973	48,382,000	26,744,000	55.3	18,649,000	38.5	2,989,000	6.2
1974	52,835,000	27,388,000	51.8	22,333,000	42.3	3,114,000	5.9
1975	56,311,000	27,433,000	48.7	24,938,000	44.3	3,940,000	7.0
1976	61,782,000	29,225,000	47.3	28,631,000	46.3	3,926,000	6.4
Percentage change 1970–76	+39.1	+4.3		+101.1		+80.4	

Source: Fritz Machlup, Kenneth W. Leeson, and associates, *Information Through the Printed Word: The Dissemination of Scholarly, Scientific, and Intellectual Knowledge* (New York. New York University, March 15, 1978; processed).

scholars face within the communication network. The concerns of scholarly book publishers regarding declining unit sales are also borne out by these data, and declining unit sales translate into higher book prices as fixed costs are spread over a smaller number of copies. And, even though library expenditures on journals have risen much faster than on books, the reports of cancelled subscriptions as library budgets tighten are a source of concern to journal publishers. Libraries in turn are forced to make difficult allocation decisions as the gap between their resources and the potential material worth acquiring grows. How are libraries coping with these increasing problems of choice? What factors determine collection development in a time of limited resources? What improvements might be made in the library decision-making process? For assistance in answering these questions, the Enquiry joined with the National Endowment for the Humanities in supporting several case studies of library-collection development, conducted by Hugh Cline and Loraine Sinnott of the Educational Testing Service. A summary of their findings is presented in the next section.

THE CLINE–SINNOTT STUDY

The project was designed to provide detailed information on collection-development policies and practices by case studies of seven academic libraries: Earlham College, Stockton State College, Brown University, Pennsylvania State University, the University of North Carolina, the University of Wisconsin, and the University of California.[11] The study involves analysis of resource allocation and of the structure and function of complex organizations. Using the methods of anthropological field research, the investigators visited each of the seven institutions over a period of ninety-two person-days. Interviews averaging sixty minutes in length were conducted with 340 academic librarians, faculty members, and college and university administrators. Interview data were supplemented with field observations and material collected from existing statistical summaries and reports.

Collection development, a phrase used to describe the variety of activities resulting in the addition to library holdings of books, serials, and other materials, usually involves library staff, faculty, and administrators. The two critical aspects of collection development are the processes of fund allocation and item selection, both of which were investigated in this study.

[11]This summary was prepared for the Enquiry by Hugh Cline and Loraine Sinnott.

Fund allocation is the process of deciding what proportion of the materials budget for a given year will be assigned to various expenditure categories, for example, the chemistry branch library, the reference department, the Slavic bibliographer, or the replacement of missing books. There is one striking common element among the seven institutions in fund allocation; when asked to explain their procedures, invariably librarians reported that monies were allocated among various funds primarily on the basis of the prior year's distribution. Minor adjustments might be made by a collection-development officer for differential inflationary factors in various scholarly fields, but in each institution there is heavy reliance upon past allocations to set the pattern for current outlays.

It is interesting to speculate why past patterns govern current allocations. There are clearly other options for allocating book funds, and library publications are replete with suggestions. One factor contributing to the reliance on the past is the financial environment within which libraries currently operate. In a period of fiscal constraint, any modification in the pattern of allocation would require cutbacks for some areas. Because library units have so many continuing commitments to journal, periodical, and other subscriptions, major reductions would affect the amount of money available for flexible spending, and perhaps force termination of continuing commitments. Thus a major redirection of financial resources would require sharp cuts for some units. Furthermore, faculty served by the units cut would probably oppose the change in policy, adding a political dimension to the problems of library management. If changes are introduced in the pattern of fund allocation, it is often administratively and politically expedient to proceed with only minor adjustments.

The seven libraries can be classified in three groups with regard to fund-allocation procedures. In the first group, one individual is responsible for allocating funds across the units. This person takes responsibility for locating necessary data such as current inflationary factors of publications within specific scholarly disciplines, and applying them to the fund allocations of the previous year. He or she may consult with library staff members, but final approval invariably is automatic. The proportion of the budget allocated to each unit, as well as the dollar amount, is not publicly announced. There is no elaborate effort to keep the figures secret, but there is apparently little interest among the library staff or the faculty in the details of specific allocations.

In the second group, funds are allocated according to a fixed set of percentages that are publicly announced. These percentages have been used for several years, and there is little expectation that they will be modified substantially in the near future.

The third group uses a faculty committee for fund allocation. Usually a library staff member presents a first draft of recommended allocations, which the committee reviews and often modifies. Testimony from library staff members or faculty may be taken concerning requests for additional funds.

The second major aspect of collection development explored in the seven case studies is *item selection*—the policies and procedures governing the expenditure of allocated funds. A variety of procedures are employed by the institutions, by item selectors within the same institution, and by the same selectors over time. Indeed, if there are twenty-five item selectors in an institution, there are at least twenty-six procedures for item selection.

Three different groups are involved in item selection: (1) library staff members, (2) faculty members, and (3) representatives of commercial vendors and publishers. Among library staff members, any one or a combination of the following may participate in item selection: library director, collection-development staff, bibliographers, branch librarians, or reference librarians. In addition, a number of libraries are diverting staff members not traditionally involved in collection development to item selection. For example, members of the cataloging department in two of the institutions have recently become involved in selection. With the expansion of shared cataloging systems, more members of cataloging departments may be assigned other duties, either on a part-time or full-time basis; and item selection is an appropriate assignment.

Faculty play both formal and informal roles in collection development. Those involved formally are designated by their colleagues as faculty–library liaisons. They work in this capacity either independently or with other colleagues in a faculty library committee. Faculty who are informally involved in collection development are individuals who are contacted by library staff members for advice concerning a potential acquisition or who submit unsolicited title requests to the library.

Representatives of commercial vendors often provide information regarding item selection, and others are given responsibility for executing decisions themselves. In addition, vendors may become involved in the actual delivery of materials to the library. There are a number of different arrangements between libraries and vendors, including standing orders, blanket orders, and approval plans. Standing orders are given to specific publishing houses, most commonly university presses and research institutes. These are permanent orders with the publisher to send one or more copies of every item published. Blanket orders are contractual agreements between libraries and jobbers, such as Baker and Taylor or Blackwell North American. In blanket orders, the library agrees to accept copies of all new titles issued by specific presses in general subject areas. Blanket orders may be given to foreign book dealers, such as Harrossowitz in Germany or the Rosenbergs in London. The approval plan is a contractual agreement with jobbers to send copies of all materials published in more narrowly defined areas. The library reviews materials sent and, if inappropriate, returns them to the jobber. (Librarians tend to use the terms *blanket order* and *approval plan* interchangeably, thereby causing confusion.)

Individuals involved in the manifold aspects of item selection rely upon a variety of tools for identifying items. There are a number of periodicals which review new publications, including *Library Journal* and *Choice*. Reviews in all the periodicals tend to be brief, and many involved in selection feel that they are too superficial. Nevertheless, they are widely used in colleges and universities.

Library of Congress proof slips of forthcoming catalog cards are also used extensively. Librarians find these helpful in alerting them to new items, especially those produced by minor publishers. National bibliographies, yet another tool used in item selection, are issued regularly to cite new publications; many librarians consider *Publishers' Weekly* a national bibliography for new domestic issues. A wide variety of other materials, such as announcements from publishers, reviews and advertisements in scholarly journals, comprehensive bibliographies within specified substantive areas, bibliographies in published articles, and the accessions lists of other academic libraries, are also used by item selectors.

Cline and Sinnott discuss a number of dilemmas presently confronting academic libraries, caused by the following conditions: the loss in the purchasing power of materials budgets due to the mounting costs of books and periodicals; stable or declining budgets as a result of constraints on growth in higher education; the explosion in the production and consumption of knowledge; and deterioration of the paper of many holdings. Amid these conditions, librarians must strive to match their holdings to the research and instructional needs of the college or university's programs, a responsibility with implications for the appropriate training and expertise required of item selectors. Finally, they point to the increasing visibility of library operations and the corresponding expectation on the part of academic administrators for a new level of accountability from these operations.

These three studies provide information about the attitudes and behavior of scholars and librarians in recent years, and about trends in library expenditure and acquisition patterns. But what of the future? We turn now to a brief discussion of the situation likely to face research libraries during the next decade, and conclude with recommendations based on that analysis.

THE PROSPECT

Of the 105 members of the Association of Research Libraries (ARL), 94 are university libraries, which suggests that the financial prospects for most research libraries will be largely determined by the economic situation of the major research universities. Indeed, a cursory look back over the past two decades shows clearly that the fortunes of libraries are closely coupled to those of the parent institutions. Universities, and higher education generally, experienced rapid growth in enrollments, staffing, and revenues from the late 1950s through the 1960s, but have been faced during the 1970s with sharply reduced rates of growth in each of these areas.[12] Library statistics, collected by the ARL and analyzed by Miriam Drake of Purdue University, point to a similar break in growth patterns in the early 1970s. For 62 libraries that reported comparable data over the period 1966–75, the ten-year (1966–75) average annual rate of growth in volumes held in the median library was 4.1 percent, but for the last five years (1971–75), the rate had dropped to 2.9 percent. A similar comparison for total expenditures produced growth rates of 8.8 percent for the ten-year period and 4.8 percent for the last five years, and for materials expenditures, rates of 6.6 percent and 0.2 percent, respectively.[13] Libraries have clearly shared in the tighter budgets and general austerity that universities have experienced in this decade.

If the resources available to research libraries continue to move in consort with the resources available to universities generally (and we do not expect this relationship to change), then the outlook for the next decade or more is for continued—and perhaps more severe—financial stringency. State university budgets tend to be enrollment-driven, while private institutions rely heavily on tuition payments; thus a leveling off in enrollments presages a leveling off of resources. The number of eighteen-year-olds in the U.S. population will decline by more than 25 percent (from 4.3 to 3.2 million) between now and the early 1990s. Whether—and to what extent—

[12] W. Vance Grant and C. George Lind, *Digest of Education Statistics, 1977–78* (Washington, D.C., GPO, 1978).
[13] Miriam A. Drake, ''Academic Research Libraries: A Study of Growth'' (Lafayette, Ind., Purdue University, February 1977; processed).

this drop in the traditional college-age population will result in enrollment declines is far from certain, but it seems safe to predict that the 1980s will witness little, if any, growth in higher-education enrollments, and certainly nothing comparable to the growth of the 1960s, or even 1970s.[14] Steady enrollments may permit some increases in real resources per student, but any gain seems likely to be marginal at best. Since a large percentage of university budgets is taken up by relatively fixed costs (tenured faculty, utilities, building maintenance), the likelihood that library budgets can increase substantially through cost savings elsewhere in the university is virtually nil. Thus, for the next decade at least, it seems realistic to assume that universities will not have the resources to increase library budgets substantially; indeed, the more likely outcome may be a steady erosion in the real resources available to libraries from their institutions.

What of other sources of support for research libraries? Might not the federal government be expected to supply the money required to maintain the strength of these national assets? Unfortunately, the checkered history of federal support for libraries, well described by Molz in a recent book, *Federal Policy and Library Support,*[15] provides little basis for assuming that the federal government will sharply increase its direct institutional support for research libraries. A new program of aid to research libraries (Title II, Part C, of the Higher Education Act) was added during the Education Amendments of 1976, and it received appropriations of $5 million in fiscal 1978 and $6 million in fiscal 1979, respectively. Libraries bid competitively for these funds, and the grants are very valuable in helping libraries to accomplish specific objectives; no library, however, can view these funds as a permanent source of direct operating support. Similarly, private foundations will continue to provide specific project grants that make possible discrete activities within the libraries, but foundations cannot be expected to underwrite normal operating costs on a continuing basis. The university budget, therefore, seems destined to remain the dominant source of support for most of the nation's research libraries.

What are the prospects for productivity or efficiency gains within the libraries? Are technological advances that promise large cost savings imminent? In their book, *Economics of Academic Libraries,*[16] Baumol and

[14] David W. Breneman and Chester E. Finn, Jr., eds., *Public Policy and Private Higher Education* (Washington, D.C., Brookings Institution, 1978), chap. 1 and 3.

[15] Redmond Kathleen Molz, *Federal Policy and Library Support* (Cambridge, Mass., MIT Press, 1976).

[16] William J. Baumol and Matityahu Marcus, *Economics of Academic Libraries* (Washington, D.C., American Council on Education, 1973).

Marcus argue that the sharply rising unit costs of library operations coupled with steadily falling unit costs of electronic data processing make the eventual adoption of electronic equipment for many library services a near certainty. Baumol and Marcus are no doubt correct in this general conclusion, but their argument remains at an abstract level since they made no attempt to survey the actual state of data processing equipment and its adaptability for library use. Nor should they be interpreted as forecasting that adoption of computer technology will give rise to large surpluses in library budgets; instead, they argue that rising costs of current procedures will eventually make the substitution of electronic procedures economically feasible, and even necessary, if costs are to be contained. There is no implication in their argument that budgetary windfalls will be the result of such substitution.

Herman Fussler has provided a more detailed look at the prospects for technological innovation in research libraries.[17] Fussler shares the Baumol and Marcus view of the inevitability of library adoption of electronic equipment and other forms of technology to reduce costs, but sums up the prospect realistically in this concluding comment:

It is unlikely that large increases in library response capabilities, services, or resources can be quickly and easily achieved at little or no incremental cost. However, over a reasonable period of time, with a well-conceived incremental development program, one may anticipate substantial improvements in capabilities and stable or even reduced unit service costs. The carrying through of such a development will require a suitable organizational structure, reduced institutional autonomy, a substantial scholarly and professional consensus on the objectives, and some wise and statesmanlike planning and implementation.[18]

Richard de Gennaro, director of libraries at the University of Pennsylvania, writing in *Library Journal,* also states a position on libraries and technology that we believe is accurate and worth repeating:

There are still some technologists who continue to predict that research libraries as we know them will soon be superseded by rapidly developing large-scale on-line, interactive data and textual access systems based on computers and telefacsimile systems, but such views no longer enjoy the vogue they once did. The lesson that has been learned after ten or fifteen years of experimentation and development is that technology alone is not going to save us, nor permit us to continue to build library collections as before, nor solve our problems by putting us out of business. Technol-

---

[17] Herman H. Fussler, *Research Libraries and Technology* (Chicago, Ill., University of Chicago Press, 1973).
   [18] Ibid., p. 79.

ogy will help in time and in very significant ways, but we should not allow its promise and glamor to keep us from coming to grips with the immediate and critical problems of exponential growth. The solution to these problems lies in the adoption of more realistic acquisitions policies and the development of more effective means of resource sharing, not only through computerized networks but also through the creation of new and improved national resource centers.[19]

It remains to ask whether the reduced growth of college and university faculties during the 1980s might not help to solve the library collection problem by reducing the amount of newly published material. Surprisingly little is known about the relationship of faculty numbers (and age distribution), and the supply of scholarly literature. A National Science Foundation (NSF) publication, *Statistical Indicators of Scientific and Technical Communication: 1960–1980*,[20] contains a chapter on the growth of scientific and technical literature in the United States, but no comparable analysis has been done for the humanities. The NSF study did find a high correlation between the number of scientists and engineers in the work force and the number of scientific and technical books and journal articles published, but a separate analysis covering faculty only was not reported. The study includes projections of the number of scientific and technical books and journals to be published in the United States through 1980; books are projected to increase from approximately 14,400 titles in 1974 (the last year for which data were available), to nearly 16,900 by 1980, while journals are projected to increase from 1,945 in 1974 to more than 2,100 in 1980. The number of scholarly scientific and technical articles published in the United States is projected to grow from approximately 150,500 in 1974 to 172,300 by 1980.[21] In all cases, the rate of growth projected from 1974 to 1980 is considerably below that experienced in the fifteen years preceding.

The scientific and technical fields differ from the humanities in that a much higher proportion of doctoral scientists and engineers is employed outside the universities; thus, the growth of scientific and technical literature is not as closely linked to faculty numbers as is the case in the humanities. The size of college and university faculties is not projected to increase during the 1980s,[22] suggesting that the growth rate in humanistic scholarly publica-

[19] Richard de Gennaro, "Austerity, Technology, and Resource Sharing: Research Libraries Face the Future," *Library Journal* (May 15, 1975) pp. 918–919.

[20] D. W. King and associates, *Statistical Indicators of Scientific and Technical Communication: 1960–1980*, vol. 1 (Washington, D.C., National Science Foundation, 1976).

[21] Ibid., chap. 3.

[22] Allan M. Cartter, *Ph.D.'s and the Academic Labor Market*, (New York, McGraw-Hill, 1976).

tion may stabilize, while the publication of scientific and technical literature will continue to grow at a modest rate roughly determined by the increased numbers of scientists and engineers. If these qualitative judgments about growth rates are broadly accurate, libraries will experience some relief from the acquisition pressures of recent years, although the volume of foreign publications and research materials such as government documents will not be affected directly by the slowdown in faculty numbers. Furthermore, as noted earlier, the same forces that will slow faculty growth will also dampen university budgets, the prime source of library operating funds. Thus, the gap between library budgets and potential acquisitions, rather than diminishing, will probably grow more severe; the economic problem of how best to allocate scarce library dollars among competing uses will become ever more pressing.

Compounding the problem of numbers of books, serials, and other materials is the rapid increase in prices of these items. The Higher Education Price Index compiled by Kent Halstead reports a remarkable increase in the book and periodical index, the figure rising from a base of 1967=100 to a level of 267.7 by 1977.[23] Of the three components of the Index, U.S. hardcover books had increased from 1967=100 to 253.5 by 1977, U.S. periodicals to 288.2, and foreign monographs to 278.6.[24] Within the total context of college and university outlays, book and periodical prices grew more rapidly between 1967 and 1977 than any other broad category of expenditure. The 1977 book and periodical index figure of 267.7 compares to indexes for personnel compensation of 187.0, supplies and materials of 180.6, equipment of 171.9, and utilities of 258.1.[25] Although the recent rapid rate of increase in utilities costs seems likely to outpace the rise in book and periodical prices in the future, there is little reason to anticipate a slowdown in book and periodical price increases; thus, libraries seem destined to face a growing volume of published material at sharply rising prices with acquisition budgets that will fail to keep pace with price and quantity increases.

It is worth noting that the price increases of scientific journals have sharply outpaced those of other fields in recent years. Clasquin and Cohen report survey results showing that price indexes for physics and chemistry journals went from 1967=100 to 1976=341.3 and 296.3, respectively, with

---

[23] D. Kent Halstead, *Higher Education Prices and Price Indexes,* 1975; and *Supplements,* 1975 and 1977 (Washington, D.C., GPO).

[24] Halstead, *Higher Education Prices and Price Indexes, 1977 Supplement,* p. 27.

[25] Ibid., p. 19.

average subscription prices per journal in 1976 of $167.71 in physics and $148.81 in chemistry.[26] These data highlight another dimension of the library dilemma facing the humanities, for the extremely high and rapidly increasing costs of scientific and technical journals mean in many cases that scholarly books in the humanities are crowded out of library budgets.

Finally, what of interlibrary loans? Does the solution to the numerous cost and acquisition problems lie in a sharp increase in the volume of such loans—in essence, a policy of resource sharing? Indeed, the number of interlibrary loans has increased steadily in recent years, with more than 2.3 million items loaned by the 105 members of the Association of Research Libraries during 1976–77.[27] The costs of interlibrary loans have been studied extensively,[28] and would be estimated at between $7 and $10 per item in 1978. Concerned with these rising costs—which deflect resources away from the institutions' direct borrowers—eight university libraries recently began charging between $3 and $8 per item loaned.[29] Other libraries impose an indirect cost on borrowers by giving interlibrary loans very low priority, extending the time between request and delivery to several weeks. Furthermore, interlibrary lending is an uncertain source for acquiring materials; since no librarian can count on being able to secure a given item by that means, it is not possible (or at least not wise) to base a library's collection and retention policies on assumed access to materials through interlibrary loans. Although the concept of resource sharing is sound, new methods for accomplishing it must be found.

CONCLUSIONS

Thus far, the discussion has supported the following conclusions:

1. Research library budgets, which in the majority of cases depend on university budgets, are unlikely to increase significantly in constant dollars over the next decade.

[26] F. F. Clasquin and Jackson B. Cohen, "Prices of Physics and Chemistry Journals," *Science* vol. 197 (29 July 1977) pp. 432–438.

[27] Suzanne Frankie (compiler), *ARL Statistics: 1976–1977* (Washington, D.C., Association of Research Libraries, 1977) p. 14.

[28] Vernon E. Palmour and associates, *A Study of the Characteristics, Costs, and Magnitude of Interlibrary Loans in Academic Libraries* (Westport, Conn., Greenwood Publishing Company, 1972); and Vernon E. Palmour and associates, "Methods of Financing Interlibrary Loan Services" (Westat, Inc., February 1974; processed).

[29] Survey conducted in 1976 by the Association of Research Libraries.

2. Neither the federal government nor private foundations are likely to provide substantial new library resources.

3. Adoption of new technology may help to slow cost increases, but will not be a source of windfall budget surpluses.

4. The lack of growth of college and university faculties during the 1980s will slow the increase of new book and journal publications, particularly in the humanities, but the gap between library budgets and potential acquisitions will not diminish, and indeed will probably grow.

5. The costs of books and periodicals have risen more rapidly than other major categories of college and university expenditure during the last decade, and seem likely to continue to do so.

6. Growing concern with the costs to the lending institution of interlibrary loans, plus the unreliability of such loans as a source of materials, mean that new methods for resource sharing must be developed.

If these conclusions are broadly accurate, then it is clear that research libraries can no longer function as autonomous entities, each striving for self-sufficiency. That goal, never realistic even in the years of rapidly expanding budgets, will slip farther out of reach as each year passes. New forms of resource sharing, the development of national collections accessible to all research libraries, and the linking of libraries through computerized bibliographic networks into a national system are essential steps that must be taken if libraries are to meet their responsibilities to provide all users with reliable access to the research literature. Our most important recommendations concentrate on the new capabilities that must be created if the system of scholarly communication is to function effectively in the years ahead.

The Enquiry's analysis of the economic situation facing research libraries and the actions needed to cope with the situation is by no means unique. The views expressed above are widely shared within the research library community, and have been expressed in one way or another by various commentators in recent years. What is unique about the present moment is the existence of a concrete plan for developing a national periodicals center, together with the beginning of a national bibliographic system linking several library consortia and state or regional networks. The will and the ability to implement changes that have heretofore remained at the discussion stage appear to be present, and this report adds the weight of representatives from all parts of the scholarly communication network in endorsing these actions. In summarizing our recommendations for a national bibliographic network, national periodicals center, and a national operating agency to oversee these developments, the implications of these changes for book and journal publishers, scholars, foundations, and government will be our prime concern.

A NATIONAL BIBLIOGRAPHIC SYSTEM

An ideal bibliographic system would permit scholars to identify information pertinent to their work and to indicate how and where that information can be most readily obtained. This ideal is far from being realized, however, even for scholars with direct access to a major research library. For those who must depend on smaller libraries, access to many existing publications is effectively foreclosed.

Fortunately, the development of computerized bibliographic systems promises to expand access to scholarly materials dramatically by freeing users from dependence on the local library collection and card catalogue as the source of information on books, serials, and other materials. A variety of bibliographic data bases have been created in recent years, covering specific fields of inquiry such as medicine and agriculture, or serving libraries in a specific state or region. The task ahead is to build upon these efforts by linking them together into an accessible bibliographic system that will serve the members of the research community, regardless of a scholar's field of study or location. Such a system will also help in the internal operations of libraries, making it possible to improve their performance.

Forging a national bibliographic system from the many elements already in existence plus the creation of new components will be a multiyear job, replete with tedious and time-consuming technical and operating details that must be worked out in a cooperative manner. A promising start has been made under the leadership of the Council of Library Resources, which, with the Library of Congress and the National Commission on Libraries and Information Science, has served as the agency to bring together a number of organizations and individuals to participate in the design and initial development of the projected bibliographic service. In announcing the new Bibliographic Service Development Program, the Council stated that:

Fundamental to future success is the fact that projected system improvement will be built on past accomplishments, including (1) the standardized data bases generated at the Library of Congress since 1968; (2) the demonstrated success of OCLC, Inc., in supplying promptly and economically millions of catalog cards to hundreds of member libraries; (3) the skills, knowledge, and techniques acquired in the process of developing sophisticated information retrieval systems at the Library of Congress, the National Library of Medicine, OCLC, Inc., the Washington State Library, Chicago, Stanford, Toronto, Northwestern, and several other universities; (4) the efforts of the Research Libraries Group, NELINET (New England Library Information Network), SOLINET (Southeastern Library Network), and others to establish new administrative and governing mechanisms suited to cooperative undertakings; (5) the growing body of accepted standards controlling record content and format that are essential to building a durable bibliographic structure in a systematic way; and (6) an improved understanding by all those involved of the work to be done and clear evidence of a willingness to participate in a cooperative undertaking of great difficulty, yet of even greater importance.[30]

Grants from private foundations and the National Endowment for the Humanities totaling over $5 million have been pledged to cover the first five years of work. The experience with this initial venture should provide guidance for the continued development and expansion of the bibliographic system. What is needed now is cooperation from other potential participants and the active involvement of scholarly societies, particularly in disciplines that have not already developed computerized bibliographic data bases. Further developmental funds will be necessary in future years as the need for additional services arises.

Furthermore, the success of on-demand publication, as discussed in previous chapters, will depend critically upon the quality and comprehensiveness of bibliographic coverage. Inclusion in a well-organized and accessible bibliographic system will be absolutely essential if material recorded or stored for distribution on-demand is to stand any chance of being identified and used. One of the benefits of the national periodicals center discussed in recommendation 4.2 would be the expansion of on-demand publication of materials that have a limited market; however, that potential will not be realized without the parallel development of a comprehensive bibliographic system. Thus, the potential benefits of a national bibliographic network can be magnified by the development of a periodicals center, both serving as component parts of an improved system for scholarly communication.

Recommendation 4.1: A national bibliographic system
We recommend that research libraries, scholarly associations, and organizations currently engaged in producing bibliographic services

---

[30] "The Bibliographic Service Development Program," Press release from the Council on Library Resources, Washington, D.C., January 17, 1979, pp. 3–4.

join with the Library of Congress in creating a linked, national bibliographic system.

A NATIONAL PERIODICALS CENTER

By enhancing the capability of scholars to identify materials relevant to
their research interests, an improved bibliographic system will increase the
borrowing requests directed to libraries. In order to meet these requests, it
will be necessary to develop more reliable and more cost-effective methods
for resource sharing. Creation of a national periodicals center promises to
meet that need for journals and other periodical publications.

Endorsed in principle by the National Commission on Libraries and
Information Science in its 1975 report,[31] the idea of a periodicals center has
been much discussed in recent years. In 1977 the Library of Congress asked
the Council on Library Resources to prepare a technical development plan
for the center, and that report was released in August 1978.[32] To become a
reality, federal legislation authorizing the creation and financing of the
center must be enacted; such legislation will probably be introduced during
the Ninety-Sixth Congress. We add our support to those who see this
legislation as essential to ensuring that the nation's research libraries can
disseminate the findings of research and scholarship effectively to all potential users.

Given the Enquiry's emphasis on effective scholarly communication,
several innovative features of this plan stand out. First, the center is not
presented as simply a large storehouse for journals and other periodical
literature, meant to serve exclusively as the source of materials for interlibrary loan. Instead, a more active role is proposed, with the center acting as
a distribution agent for publishers of certain types of materials. Second, the
national periodicals center will ensure that all copied material is delivered in
full compliance with the copyright laws, thus relieving libraries of some of
the requirements established by the CONTU (National Commission on New
Technological Uses of Copyrighted Works) guidelines. Third, a price
schedule will be established for each item, taking into account such factors
as its copyright status, age, and the frequency with which it is requested. The
fees charged will be used in part to compensate publishers for any legally

---

[31] National Commission on Libraries and Information Science, *Toward a National Program for Library and Information Services: Goals for Action* (Washington, D.C., GPO 1975).
[32] Council on Library Resources, Inc., *A National Periodicals Center: Technical Development Plan* (Council on Library Resources, 1978; processed).

required copyright fees or possible sales fees. Fourth, the existence of this facility will open new possibilities for expanded on-demand publication as an alternative to publishing new journals in areas of limited readership. It will also provide an opportunity for existing journals to experiment with synoptic or abstract publication, with full text available on demand from the national periodicals center. Fifth, the center will provide librarians with the option of relying on it for little-used material, rather than subscribing to the journal or relying solely on interlibrary loan. And, most important, its existence will expand access to the full range of research materials to scholars and all others who are not located at major universities.

Since there has been misunderstanding of the proposal for a national periodicals center, it needs to be stressed that the center will *not* give rise to wholesale cancellations by libraries of journal subscriptions. There is simply no substitute in the scholarly process for browsing through current journals as a stimulus to thought and further research, and librarians are as aware of that fact as are faculty members. Whether the center is created or not, however, the fact remains that financial pressures will continue to force librarians to exercise greater selectivity over journal acquisitions and retention. In the absence of the center, the ability of libraries to serve the needs of scholars efficiently and effectively will steadily erode. Its existence will allow librarians to develop local collections of maximum value to users, secure in the knowledge that a reliable source exists for acquiring back issues and seldom-used items.

In order to provide a better understanding of the proposed method of operation and finance of the national periodicals center, and particularly its relation to the publishing community, the summary of the technical development plan is appended to this chapter.

Recommendation 4.2:   A national periodicals center
   We recommend the establishment of a national periodicals center and endorse the plan for its development, operation, management, and financing prepared by the Council on Library Resources.

A NATIONAL LIBRARY AGENCY

Although libraries have been growing at exponential rates in recent decades, the rapid growth in cost and volume of publications means that each library is becoming increasingly less able to satisfy the research and educational needs of its users. The linking together of library resources through a nationwide bibliographic network, and the creation of a national facility, the periodicals center, are two of the responses necessary to create a capacity greater than any individual library can offer, and both are steps toward a purposefully created national library system. Additional components of this system will need to be developed, including a coordinated approach to preservation of materials and the identification and division of responsibility for maintaining (or creating) national collections. An operating agency with the mandate and funds to encourage the development of these components of a library system is necessary if the effort is to succeed.

In advancing this recommendation, we acknowledge the important and continuing role of the Library of Congress, but also recognize the need for a separate agency able to undertake and concentrate resources on new activities required by the nation's library system. These activities, which are not fully included in the current Library of Congress mandate, are development and management of the national periodicals center, development and operation of a nationwide bibliographic system, and implementation of a preservation program for deteriorating books and other scholarly materials. The new agency would work closely with the Library of Congress—which is central to the national library system—and with the nation's research libraries and others in carrying out these new functions. Without such an agency, specifically charged with accomplishing these tasks, the chances are great that the activities will not be implemented in a timely fashion.

A national periodicals center would be the first operating program of a national library agency. The center is inseparably linked, however, to the nation's bibliographic structure, the evolving library communications network, and the complex processes of resource development and preservation. The purposes of a national library agency should therefore include the following:

- To coordinate bibliographic control for the significant scholarly and research material of the world so that library patrons, scholars, and research personnel are not restricted in their work only to publications in their own libraries
- To facilitate the development, dissemination, and acceptance of national and international standards for bibliographic description and communications and for networking
- To ensure access, through lending or reproduction consistent with applicable laws, to published information of all kinds and formats which are needed by scholars but which their libraries are unable to acquire or retain

- To ensure a program for the preservation of published information through conservation techniques and maintenance of depositories for infrequently used materials in order that the accumulated experience, knowledge, and literature of the past will not be lost.

A national library agency should be governed by a body with the responsibility and authority to establish, fund, coordinate, operate, or contract for the programs and services required to carry out the purposes of the agency, to determine operating policies, and to evaluate and review management performance. The governing body should be designed, and its membership selected, with the same sensitivity to the subject of government presence which has shaped the character of the governing boards of the National Science Foundation and the National Endowments for the Arts and Humanities. Persons nominated should be drawn from the ranks of scholars, scientists, university trustees and officers, head librarians, publishers, and public figures with demonstrated broad intellectual interests.

Of course, a national library agency would have no prescriptive authority over the activities of the nation's libraries. The agency should be limited to organizing and directing national services to augment local capabilities, and to cooperative efforts that permit individual libraries to operate more effectively and efficiently.

Recommendation 4.3: A national library agency
We recommend that a new organization be created to help plan and bring about the purposeful development of a national library system.

PRESERVATION OF LIBRARY MATERIALS

The use of acids in paper manufacture during the last 150 years has resulted in deterioration—literally crumbling—of substantial portions of the country's most distinctive collections. If no action is taken, hundreds of thousands of books will simply be lost forever.

The Library of Congress has contributed to the search for ways to prevent the continued deterioration of collections and to the development of a national plan for the preservation of library materials. What is needed is not the preservation of all items in all libraries, but the certainty that no works are lost in their entirety. A systematic and coordinated program of filming deteriorating volumes will be an essential part of any preservation effort. Decisions will then have to be made regarding the storage site and bibliographic entry for the filmed items, so that scholars can locate them and receive photocopies or microform versions on demand.

The discussion above should make apparent the natural linkages of a preservation program that involves extensive micrographics to the national periodicals center, bibliographic system, and national library agency. Copies of all filmed materials might logically be stored at the center, entered in the bibliographic system, and delivered on demand to users anywhere. For these reasons, the preservation program should be a main component of the national library agency. Action on preservation cannot await creation of that agency, however, since thousands of books have already been lost, and hundreds of thousands more are so fragile that the next use will be their last. Thus, the Library of Congress must continue in a leadership role until the new operating agency is in place.

Recommendation 4.4: Preservation of library materials
We recommend that the federal government and private foundations give urgent attention to the preservation problems faced by research libraries. Leadership should be exercised by the Library of Congress until the proposed national library agency is created.

SUPPORT FOR RESEARCH COLLECTIONS
During the Education Amendments of 1976, a new program of support for research libraries (Title II, Part C) was added to the Higher Education Act of 1965. Congress appropriated $5 million for fiscal 1978 and $6 million for fiscal 1979 under this provision, with grants awarded competitively on the basis of project proposals. The first round of awards involved grants to twenty institutions, including twelve university libraries, and to such other organizations as the New York Public Library, the Boston Public Library, the Missouri Botanical Garden, the Art Institute of Chicago, the Folger Shakespeare Library, the American Museum of Natural History, the Henry E. Huntington Library and Art Gallery, and the New York State Education Department.[33]

This program should continue to be used creatively to foster the general objectives for collection development, preservation, and accessibility that the preceding recommendations are intended to achieve. Priority should be given to proposals that promise to develop (or preserve) a distinctive collection that enhances in important ways the nation's research resources. Emphasis should also be given to proposals that expand access to such collec-

[33] Office of Libraries and Learning Resources, Office of Education, "FY/78 Abstracts: Strengthening Research Library Resources Program" (Washington, D.C., U.S. Office of Education, August 1978; processed).

tions, whether through bibliographic improvements or through preservation, including filming or microforms. Each grant should be judged by its contribution to enhanced national (or regional) collections of research value, and the program should be viewed as complementing the national periodicals center, which is a unique form of national collection. Under no circumstances should the program be allowed to slip into general support of research libraries, to be allocated on other than a competitive basis.

Directed to the ends suggested above, this federal program of support for research collections will play an important part in a national strategy for library development. The program clearly should be reauthorized and fully funded.

Recommendation 4.5: Support for research collections
We recommend the reauthorization of Title II, Part C, of the Higher Education Act of 1965, as amended in 1976, which provides federal support for distinctive research collections.

THE LIBRARIANS' EDUCATIONAL RESPONSIBILITIES

The next decade will usher in many changes in the services available from libraries and in the methods of library use. Most of these changes will accelerate the trend away from each library being a self-contained unit, toward a system in which the library will be a service center, capable of linking users to national bibliographic files and distant collections. As the scholars' survey and the Cline–Sinnott studies have shown, however, these new directions in library development will initially be resisted by many faculty members and other researchers who place great weight on local self-sufficiency. It will be essential to the success and acceptance of the new approaches, therefore, for librarians on every campus to explain the reasons for the changes, the methods for using the new services, and the benefits to be derived. Faculty members also have a responsibility to learn the new techniques for library usage and to pass this knowledge along to students.

Certain educational materials could most efficiently be developed centrally, perhaps by the professional library associations. These items should be supplemented locally with information unique to each library. Campus seminars at the beginning of each term may be useful, with more attention paid to the techniques of library usage as a part of undergraduate and graduate education in all fields.[34] Librarians must exercise leadership in

[34]Cline and Sinnott describe a particularly effective program in education for library use at Earlham College in Richmond, Indiana.

bringing these issues to the fore in campus discussion, and must see library education as a growing part of their jobs.

Recommendation 4.6: The librarians' educational responsibilities
We recommend that librarians, together with faculty members, play an active role in educating students and other library users to the changes in services and procedures that can be expected in future years.

APPENDIX: SUMMARY OF THE TECHNICAL DEVELOPMENT PLAN FOR A NATIONAL PERIODICALS CENTER
In the fall of 1977, the Library of Congress (LC) asked the Council on Library Resources (CLR) to prepare a technical development plan for a U.S. national periodicals center (NPC). The need for such a facility was formalized by the National Commission on Libraries and Information Science in its 1977 document *Effective Access to Periodical Literature,* which recommended that the Library of Congress assume responsibility for developing, managing, and operating the center. LC and the council agreed that the plan would be prepared in such a way that it could be used by the Library or any other agency prepared to assume responsibility for the creation of a major periodicals facility. Several foundations contributed to the cost of preparing the plan, which was completed in August 1978.

The goal of the national periodicals center is to improve access to periodical literature for libraries and thus to individuals using libraries. The intent of the plan is to assure that the NPC will accomplish this goal (1) by providing an efficient, reliable, and responsive document-delivery system for periodical material; (2) by working effectively with the publishing community; and (3) by helping to shape a national library system through NPC operating policies and procedures.

The specific operating objectives of the NPC follow logically from this goal and are:

1. To provide a reliable method of access to a comprehensive collection of periodical literature.

2. To reduce the overall costs of acquiring periodical material by interlibrary loan (ILL).

NOTE: This appendix has been reprinted from the Council on Library Resources, *A National Periodicals Center: Technical Development Plan* (Council on Library Resources, 1978; processed).

3. To reduce the time required to obtain requested material.

4. To assure that for any document delivered through the NPC, all required copyright fees and obligations will have been paid.

5. To act, under appropriate conditions, as a distribution agent for publishers.

6. To provide libraries with additional options as they establish their own collection development and maintenance policies.

7. To promote the development of local and regional resource sharing.

8. To contribute to the preservation of periodical material.

9. To provide a base for the development of new and imaginative publication strategies.

10. To provide a working example of a national access service that might be extended to other categories of materials.

These operating objectives make it clear that the national periodicals center will link in new ways the collecting and distribution functions of libraries with the distribution activities of at least some kinds of publishing. The center's governance must also be approached in a new, imaginative way, one that will assure close coordination between its operation and the development of other national programs (e.g., bibliographic control, communications, etc.) that together will constitute the foundation of a national library and information system. But the present library and information structure of the nation is composed of many discrete components. This fact, together with the complexity of library functions and the dispersion of library services, makes it unlikely that there will or should be a formal prescriptive central-ized agency charged with operating a single hierarchical national library system.

What seems required, as the plan suggests, is a two-tier structure at the national level. This would involve the creation of a new organization with authority and funds to establish and coordinate the few fundamental programs that are best handled at the national level. The separate governing bodies of these programs would constitute the second tier. The first operating responsibility of a coordinating agency (a kind of national library board) would be to establish the periodicals center whose governing body would be responsible to the board through an executive director's office. This proposed governance structure, though an integral part of the plan, does not pre-determine the specifications for the NPC itself.

As proposed in the plan, the national periodicals center will contain a central-ized collection of periodical literature directly accessible to libraries throughout the nation. Initially projected at 36,000 titles, subscriptions for which would be gener-ated as quickly as possible, the collection would continue to grow prospectively (adding more titles) and retrospectively (acquiring back files) according to an established strategy and in as timely a fashion as possible. All subject areas would be included with the initial exception of clinical medicine. Eventually the collection may number in excess of 60,000 current titles, but it will never contain all of the estimated 200,000 currently published periodicals. Though few of those not held by the NPC are likely to be in great demand, it is planned that the NPC would provide access to many of them through a system of referral libraries. The NPC will contract with referral libraries to provide service to requesting libraries that desire specific titles not in the NPC collection. All requests would be channeled through the NPC to assure uniformity of procedure and to provide the means to monitor system performance.

The NPC will develop and make available a finding tool to identify the titles and holdings to which the NPC can provide access. The finding tool will be organized by key title and International Standard Serial Number (ISSN) and will include titles available from both the NPC collection and the referral system libraries. For the first several years libraries will be required to request only material listed in the tool. Each order will have to include the ISSN or an NPC-generated substitute number and the key title.

The most important question for many librarians is which libraries will be able to go directly to the NPC. After a break-in period for the NPC and after the collection is well established, all libraries will have access. The decision to use the NPC or alternatives such as local, state, or regional resources should be based upon the actual dollar cost of the transaction and the reliability of access or delivery.

Several fiscal considerations will aid libraries in making these sorts of decisions. First, any library or consortium wishing to have access to the NPC will be required to establish a deposit account equal to the institution's expected request activity for one month, with some arbitrary minimum required. Second, a price schedule will be established that takes into account the copyright status of a particular item, its age, and the frequency with which it is requested. All NPC transactions will require the payment of a fee, part of which will be used to defray any legally required copyright fees or possible sales fees. Librarians using the NPC will be assured that for any item received from the center, the appropriate fees will have been paid. This will relieve libraries of some of the requirements established by the CONTU (National Commission on New Technological Uses of Copyrighted Works) guidelines.

Quite apart from the procedures to comply with the copyright legislation, it is imperative in the interest of effective scholarly communication that the NPC develop effective relationships with the publishing community. It is proposed that the NPC become a kind of service and fulfillment outlet for at least some publishers. Thus the NPC might provide a back-issue service (probably in microform), an article sales service (so long as the article remained protected by copyright), an outlet for on-demand publishing, and/or a source for the full text of material published in synoptic form. All of these services would generate some income for publishers while providing the access to material that library users need. It is recognized that a relationship of this kind may tend to modify traditional information production and/or distribution functions. But each element of the information chain has a unique and valuable role to play in serving the needs of inquiring scholars, and each must be supportive of the other.

The internal structure of the NPC will be organized to achieve fast internal processing so that requests will be filled within twenty-four hours of receipt. Much of the most active collection will be stored in microfiche because this is the fastest request-fulfillment mode of storage. Other less heavily used materials will be stored in their original form and retrieved for photoduplication. Most requests will be filled with paper photocopy; microfiche will also be available at an enticing discount.

Requests will be handled in as simple and direct a manner as possible. Libraries will be encouraged to transmit requests to the NPC in electronic form so they can be received, verified, and forwarded to the fill site by machine. For items not in the NPC collection, the machine system will batch and transmit requests on a scheduled basis to appropriate referral sites. "Picking slips" for requests to be filled at the NPC will be automatically generated and directed to the appropriate storage site for fulfillment. After copies are made they will be packaged—probably in a plastic wrapper with the picking slip now used as the address label. First-class mail will be used to send most requests. Other rapid-transport systems (air freight/express) may be used to move mail into the U.S. Postal Service's one-day delivery zones. Some institutions with the capacity to receive material via facsimile transmission may choose to pay the higher costs of this delivery mechanism.

A peripheral but nonetheless vital objective of the NPC is to participate in the national preservation program. Consequently, all materials received by the center will be handled in such a way as to assure access for as long as possible. The costs of preservation are high but must be assumed as part of the effort to provide effective access to periodical literature in perpetuity.

The cost of the NPC must eventually be covered by a combination of federal subsidy and user fees. However, the start-up costs must be fully subsidized for at least the first three years. First-year costs will be $3,750,000 and will cover the basic organization of the NPC and the first-year collection costs. Second-year costs rise to $4,850,000 and cover the costs of the second-year collection development effort as well as the costs of bringing all systems up to an operational level. Third-year costs rise to $5,450,000 and are only minimally offset by transaction receipts. This year is a break-in year for all operating systems and as such is expected to produce only marginal levels of activity and therefore income. Beyond the fourth year (basic operating cost $1,925,000) costs will become more directly related to the level of request fulfillment activity. However, in order to achieve full preservation microfilming, a $3,000,000 subsidy is required in year four. The annual subsidy should then decline as request-fulfillment activity and income rises in each succeeding year.

The site of the NPC is dependent upon the quality of all relevant and available communications systems, availability of power and other utility services, and an adequate pool of manpower. The plan recommends new construction in order to avoid reducing the efficiency of NPC functions by forcing them into inappropriate spaces. The cost of construction for a building for the NPC should be $5.5–6.5 million for 130,000 net square feet. Construction funds should be available during the first year. Construction should proceed fairly rapidly since the building required is a simple modular warehouse facility. The most complicated features of the structure relate to the specific environmental requirements.

Upon acceptance of the technical development plan, three separate kinds of activity should proceed simultaneously. The first involves the establishment of a legal basis and funding support for a national library board, the first operating responsibility of which would be the national periodicals center. Second, a senior executive with necessary secretarial and travel support should be charged with the responsibility of explaining the plan for an NPC to the library, publishing, and scholarly communities. This individual would provide a focus for the comments and suggestions that are bound to be generated by the circulation of the technical development plan. The third activity, which will require establishing a core of two or three permanent NPC staff, is to continue the detailed planning for the NPC, including identification of first-year titles, identification of appropriate back files, identification of any existing computer operating systems that might be appropriate for anticipated NPC activities, and the preparation of specifications for systems that will be required. These are important tasks that would accomplish two things: (1) provide a running start for the NPC operation and (2) demonstrate to the Congress that the library community is serious about and committed to a national periodicals center.

The creation of a national periodicals center will require the cooperative action and support of librarians, information scientists, publishers, politicians, foundation managers, and the eventual NPC staff itself. One thing is clear. Society has everything to gain from an improved capacity to retrieve and use the information generated by its members. A coherent national periodicals program should provide such an improvement. A national periodicals center is the first step.

Afterword

From our own conversations, and from the initial reactions of outside readers, we know that several of our proposals—and the lines of reasoning that support them—are controversial, and we anticipate debate over their merits. Indeed, some of the most active discussion—both pro and con—will no doubt be led by members of the Enquiry's governing board. One of our main purposes will have been served, however, if the report stimulates further thought and leads to improved understanding of the challenges facing the system of scholarly communication.

If, however, the report does no more than stimulate debate or research and does not lead to action, it will have failed in its principal purpose. The proposals for change advanced here need to be tested by thoroughgoing discussion, but those that survive this test (and we think most will), are not automatically assured of implementation. They will be put into practice only if they are given the support of scholars, journal editors, publishers, librarians, and officials of universities, scholarly societies, foundations, and governments.

Our concern for action is reflected in three of the recommendations in chapter 1, noted here for emphasis. We have sought to create a continued capacity for change and adaptation within the scholarly system through the auspices of the National Library Agency (Recommendation Three), the Office of Scholarly Communication (Recommendation Eleven), and the joint committee of scholars, publishers, and librarians (Recommendation Twelve). We have no doubt that the problems facing scholarly communication—and their potential solutions—will continue to change, and we believe that these new agencies will provide a valuable capacity for promoting analysis and action. The modest investment in institutional capability proposed in these three recommendations should yield rich dividends in the form of a more adaptable and responsive system for scholarly communication.

Despite the number of recommendations contained in this report, we recognize that many questions have been only lightly explored—notably the consequences of the emphasis on publication as a major criterion for academic advancement. This question, which we encountered in many contexts, is at the root of many communication problems, but it transcends communication and needs to be addressed by the scholarly community at large.

A central question that has concerned us throughout the study is, What should be expected of the scholarly community itself and what should be expected from private foundations and government, which are outside that community but are essential participants in the system of scholarly communication? Our conclusion—embodied in numerous recommendations—is that the scholarly community must be continually challenged to demonstrate that it is performing efficiently and that it is seeking to develop new forms of self-help. We also conclude, however, that the performance of the scholarly community overall justifies greater support by government and private foundations. We urge that they consider our recommendations carefully in deciding how they can best contribute to the development of the scholarly enterprise. Their continued backing will be indispensable.

Appendix: Principal Studies Commissioned by the National Enquiry

PUBLISHED STUDIES

1. Nazir A. Bhagat and Robert A. Forrest, "How Many Copies Should We Print?," *Scholarly Publishing* (October 1977).
2. John J. Corson, "How University Administrators View University Presses," *Scholarly Publishing* (January 1978).
3. August Frugé, "Beyond Publishing: a System of Scholarly Writing and Reading," *Scholarly Publishing* (July 1978 and October 1978).

UNPUBLISHED STUDIES

1. Hugh F. Cline and Loraine T. Sinnott, "Organization Case Studies of Collection Development Policies and Practices" (Educational Testing Service, February 1979, processed).
2. Joan Eckstein, "A Report on the Business Committee for the Arts" (National Enquiry into Scholarly Communication, May 1977, processed).
3. Bernard M. Fry and Herbert S. White, "Impact of Economic Pressures on American Libraries and Their Decisions Concerning Scholarly and Research Journal Acquisition and Retention" (Washington, D.C., National Science Foundation, Division of Science Information, June 1978, processed).
4. Janet D. Griffith, "The Survey of Scholars: Relationships Between the Scholars and Other Estates," An analysis and presentation of the results of the survey planned and conducted by the staff of the National Enquiry. (Research Triangle Park, N.C., Research Triangle Institute, February 1978, processed).
5. Simone Reagor and W. S. Brown, "The Application of Advanced Technology to Scholarly Communication in the Humanities" (National Enquiry into Scholarly Communication, June 1978, processed).
6. Datus C. Smith, Jr., "Foundations and Scholarly Publishing," (National Enquiry into Scholarly Communication, December 1977, processed).
7. Datus C. Smith, Jr., "Foreign Distribution of American University Press Books" (National Enquiry into Scholarly Communication, June 1977, processed).

Index